Art As Design: Design As Art
A Contemporary Guide

Sterling McIlhany

VNR Van Nostrand Reinhold Company/New York
Studio Vista/London

Van Nostrand Reinhold Company Regional Offices:
New York   Cincinnati   Chicago   Millbrae   Dallas

Van Nostrand Reinhold Company Foreign Offices:
Toronto   London   Melbourne

Library of Congress Catalog Card Number 69-15898

Published simultaneously in Canada by
D. Van Nostrand Company (Canada), Ltd.

Designed by Milton Glaser
Printed by Halliday Lithograph Corporation
Color printed by Princeton Polychrome Press
Bound by Publishers Book Bindery

Published in the United States of America
by Van Nostrand Reinhold Company
450 West 33rd Street, New York, N.Y. 10001
and in Great Britain by Studio Vista Limited
Blue Star House, Highgate Hill, London N.19

16 15 14 13 12 11 10 9 8 7 6 5 4 3 2 1

Contents

Art and design today are as varied, fascinating, and sometimes confusing as the world we live in. Never before in man's long history have so many people created and designed such a vast array of objects. More paintings and sculptures are made today than were created during the Renaissance.

In one field of modern creativity every one of us is involved in a revolution more powerful and far reaching than any other taking place today. This field, the media of communication, including films, all graphic art, and, most importantly, television, is the most powerful force in the changes that are daily taking place and that directly affect the lives of everyone, educated or uneducated, young or old. The average adult will pass from ten to fifteen years watching television.

Art and serious design are not just static bodies of material preserved intact and taught without reference to the rest of reality. Students often know more about what is happening than teachers do. By high school many young people talk easily about psychedelic art, multimedia, and happenings, ideas that are foreign to many adults, including educators. One fact is clear: art is important as it never has been before. We cannot think of art as merely a good thing to know about, a refined adjunct to the real problems of living. Art is no longer to be found only in galleries and museums. The art developing today, much of it in the hands of young people, is a central life style.

The four spiral forms reproduced in the Introduction, a spiral galaxy, Chambered Nautilus, human thumbprint, and ancient capital, are stunningly far apart in function; yet they illustrate clearly the close design relationship that can exist between nature, man, and the artist.

1
Spiral Galaxy. Its distance from the earth is about two million light years. (Offiicial U.S. Navy photograph.)

2
Shell of Chambered Nautilus sectioned to show internal chambers. (Photograph courtesy The American Museum of Natural History.)

The visions created by today's professional painters and sculptors are extraordinary. Anyone even casually interested in contemporary art can feel overwhelmed by the numerous and sometimes conflicting styles that characterize art today. They are an index of the variety and cross-purpose that underlie every aspect of modern life. Yet they evidence great vitality and inventiveness, as rewarding as they are nervewracking.

The average person who does not even spend time in art galleries and museums is daily in contact with the creative work of designers and artists. The buildings we live and work in, the posters and magazines we read, the cars we ride in, and the clothes we wear are designed by talents who are expressing their own imagination and the time they live in. To people in the future the telephone and the jet airplane may be as revealing and symbolic of our age as the most sophisticated work of our fine artists. Yet they are so familiar to most people that they are taken for granted as inevitable facts of modern reality.

The chapters that follow are organized to illustrate the contemporary relationship of art and design and to create for the reader a broad view of the variety and meaning of our visual world.

3
Human thumbprint.

4
Greek marble Ionic capital. IV century B.C. (The Metropolitan Museum of Art, Gift of the American Society for the Exploration of Sardis, 1926.)

1. The Jet — Supersonic Symbol

The jet aircraft is the most compelling form of our time. Its clean tapered shape, swept-back wing and tail assembly, and thrusting engines symbolize perfectly the forces — time and space — that affect the thoughts and actions of every one of us. Anyone wishing to experience in capsule the impact of the dynamic time we live in has only to pay the price of a ticket, fasten his ·seat belt, and feel the tremendous thrust of the roaring jets as they pull the screaming craft off the runway and send it soaring into the open air. Speed, noise, and raw power, while perhaps not comforting, are basic — and, to some, exciting — facts of modern life.

The jet aircraft is so forceful a symbol that its design exerts a strong control over the shape of almost every object, regardless of use, made today. Sports cars boast "flight decks" and "jet-away" styling (and, until recently, tail fins); gas ranges, automatic dryers, food blenders, and TV sets bear the spare, aerodynamic stamp of the jet; even ashtrays and lamps appear ready to abandon the coffee table and take to the air. The overworked term "functional," often as not, is merely a cover word for the lean styles created originally on the aeronautical engineer's drawing board. Many of the designs illustrated throughout this book — including paintings and posters, automobiles, chairs, buildings, and clothes — owe their appearance to our contemporary preoccupation with the weightlessness, speed, and "minimal" form dictated by aircraft design.

Every age can be characterized by a single vital form that acts as a symbol for its energy and aspirations. Throughout most of history, ideals have found expression in works of art: architecture, sculpture, and painting. Since ancient times — and until very recently — architecture has acted as "mother of the arts," gathering to itself the varied talents of designers, engineers, sculptors, and painters. The history of architecture, more than any other art, is the record of man's attitudes towards himself, the world he lives in, and his relation to the life of the spirit. If we had nothing left to us but the Great Pyramids of Gizeh, the Parthenon, the Colosseum, Chartres Cathedral, and the palaces of Florence, we would still possess a deep insight into the life and thought of Ancient Egypt, Greece, and Rome, Medieval France, and Renaissance Italy.

Today, architecture is less concerned with art than it is with engineering and the exploitation of new materials. The time-battered remains of a DC-9 jet airliner would speak far more vividly centuries from now of our fast-moving, constantly changing world than any building erected in the last thirty years.

To understand this basic shift from the monumental, permanent art of architecture to the soaring, gravity-defying science of jet aircraft — and to orient our vision to the examples which follow — the illustrations in this chapter compare two key achievements of two extraordinary eras: the Renaissance Palazzo Strozzi, built in the fifteenth century in Florence, Italy, and today's jet airliner. Each expresses eloquently the spirit of the people who created it.

The Palazzo Strozzi, built in 1450 as the imposing city residence of a noble Florentine family, is one of the great landmarks of Renaissance architecture. The classical proportions of its three tall stories and the elegant refinement of its details, notably the finely carved cornice and the gracefully arched windows, project a feeling of strength, serenity, and permanence. (Photographs courtesy Alinari, Florence.)

The modern jet transport is the design symbol of our time. It is a shape born of flight. Its over-all form and finely sculptured details, like those of the Palazzo Strozzi, express the ideals of its time: in the case of the jet, weightlessness, speed, and mobility. (Photographs courtesy of Douglas Aircraft Co., Inc.; B.O.A.C.; Pan American.)

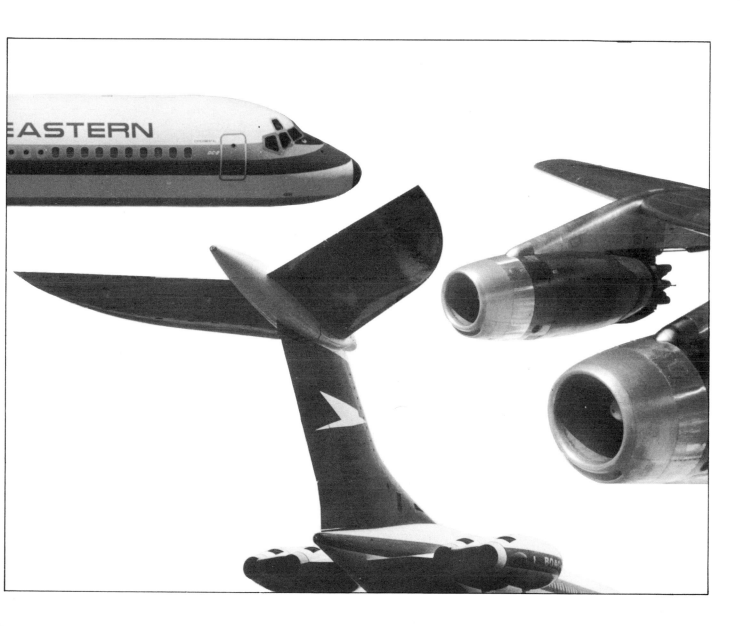

13

"Mr. Watson, come here; I want you!" With this historic command, the first complete sentence transmitted by telephone, Alexander Graham Bell signaled a revolution in the life of America and the world. Bell's telephone, patented in 1876, was but one of many extraordinary inventions of the nineteenth century. Others include — for better or worse — photography, the locomotive, the machine gun, the telegraph, the typewriter, the phonograph, the incandescent light, the movie machine, the X ray, and dynamite — as well as linoleum, oleomargarine, and the safety pin.

The first telephone, the liquid transmitter of 1876, linked pairs of users for a length of only a few miles. At first, nineteenth-century home owners took a rather dim view of the telephone, regarding it as a noisy intruder that placed the household at the unwanted mercy of the outside world. By the 1960s, however, every man, woman, and child in the United States averaged at least one conversation daily over more than 68,000,000 telephones. For many business executives and teen-agers the telephone has become the chief means of communicating with other people.

The pictures on the following pages trace the remarkable history of telephone design from the first crude models which transmitted the miracle of faint, scratchy, but recognizable vocal sounds to today's sleek direct-dial instruments with pushbuttons.

The rapid evolution of the telephone, from its invention to the present day, follows a fascinating but not unusual pattern. In the earliest stages of their development, all man-made forms — whether works of art such as sculpture and painting or useful objects like the telephone — bear the marks of their birth: bold form, strong outline, ready admission of their function.

There is little idea of self-conscious "style" to mask the stark appearance of the object itself. The first telephones, pictured on page 15, are undisguised machines, the shapes of technology during its early, or archaic, stage. The model of 1876 used the same device for talking and listening, held to the mouth or ear as required.

As the telephone developed greater technical sophistication, it lost its earlier "laboratory" look. With the magneto wall set of 1882 and the desk sets of 1892 and 1897, the telephone evolved into a refined household appliance. The elegant model of 1897 was made of cast brass.

In 1928, with the introduction of the "French phone" (so-called because it resembled European models), telephone design reached a classical peak: a graceful combination of function (receiver and transmitter combined) and subtle, flowing form. In the spirit of classical sculpture, the elegant shape suggests an ideal balance between movement and repose.

The desk sets that follow reflect changing design concepts. By 1937 the telephone — like automobiles of that time — abandons its classic sculptural grace for a more massive, angular shape. Following World War II, in the early fifties — again reflecting parallel developments in automotive design — the telephone loses its angularity, swells outward, and, in the "500" series, appears in a variety of "decorator" colors: white, beige, green, pink, and blue. Characteristic, too, of this later, baroque design phase is the proliferation, by the late fifties and during the 1960s, of a whole array of telephone models: desk sets, wall sets, the "Princess" phone, and the "Trimline."

If the design evolution of the telephone continues

the pattern it has followed so far (early or archaic stage, middle or classical stage, and late or baroque stage), two possible further developments can be predicted: the return to a severe archaic design, recalling the bold shapes of the early models (and already observable in the 1962 panel phone on page 19), and an eventual disappearance of the telephone as we know it now. Perhaps the two-way wrist communicator envisioned years ago in "Dick Tracy," and now a possibility, will be the new, strapped-on telephone of the future. (Photographs of telephones from Bell Telephone Laboratories.)

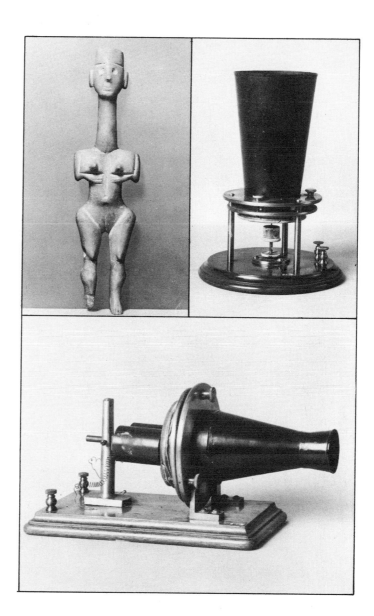

1
Archaic geometric marble statuette from the Cyclades. 3000-2000 B.C. (The Metropolitan Museum of Art, Rogers Fund, 1945.)

The first telephones (1876-1880) are expressions of pure technology. Like the earliest forms of sculpture, they are bold and symmetrical, with clear, geometric outlines and little detail.

2
1876 Liquid telephone.

3
1876 Bell's centennial model.

4
1877 First commercial telephone.

5
1878 Butterstamp.

6
1880 Blake.

7
Late archaic limestone statue from Cyprus. 600-550 B.C. (The Metropolitan Museum of Art, The Cesnola Collection, purchased by subscription, 1874-76.)

The telephones reproduced here (1882-1910) develop more graceful forms and, in the desk sets, a naturalistic detail characteristic of late archaic sculpture.

8
1882 Magneto wall set.

9
1886 Long-distance transmitter.

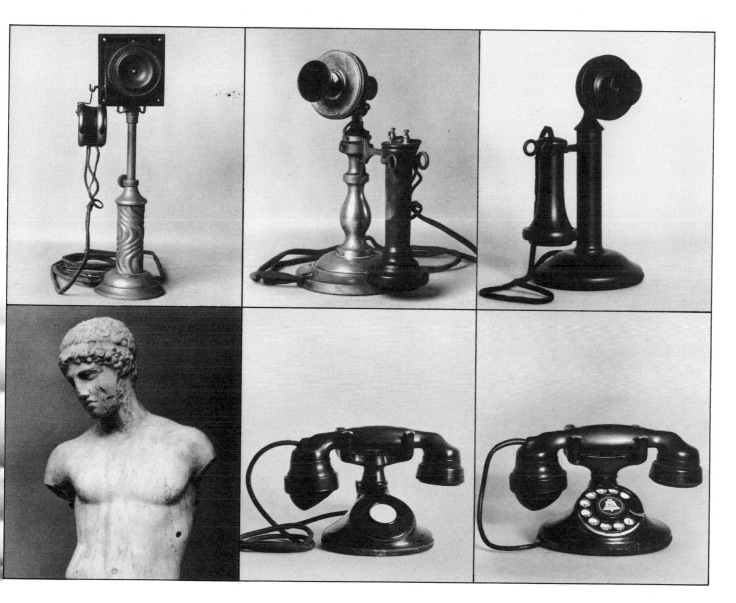

10
1892 Desk set.

11
1897 Desk set.

12
1910 Desk set.

13
Classical Greek statue
(Roman marble copy).
450-425 B.C. (The Metro-
politan Museum of Art,
Fletcher Fund, 1926.)

The familiar desk set telephone (1928-1954) is a
harmonious unity of func-
tion and beautiful form.
Its flowing outline and
sculptural detail relate it
closely to classical art.

14
1928 Desk set.

15
1930 Desk set.

16
1937 "300" desk set.

17
1949 "500" desk set.

18
1954 "500" color desk set.

19
Baroque marble portrait bust by Alessandro Algardi. Seventeenth century. (The Metropolitan Museum of Art, Louisa Eldridge McBurney Gift Fund, 1953.)

The contemporary telephones illustrated here (1956–   ) show the wide variety of forms and the swelling outlines which are found in the late, or baroque, development of sculpture.

20
1956 Wall telephone.

21
1958 Call-director telephone.

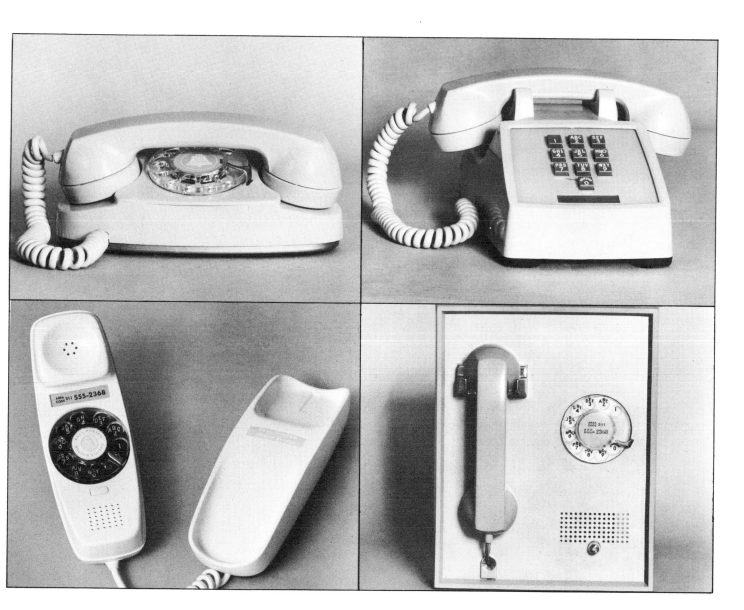

22
1959 Princess telephone.

23
1964 Touch-tone telephone.

24
1965 Trimline telephone.

25
1962 Panel phone.

The panel phone marks a return in design to the severely geometric shapes of the first telephones on page 16. It is also clearly related to the stark, unadorned "minimal" forms illustrated in Chapter 5.

3. The Fine Arts

Along with every other important field of human concern — including education, science, religion, and government — art has undergone sweeping changes in the twentieth century. Hardly anyone — neither critics, teachers, nor artists themselves — can any longer agree on what is art and what is not.

Traditionally, the term "fine art" referred to three clearly defined fields: architecture, painting, and sculpture. As we have already noted, architecture is more concerned with engineering than it is with art. It is discussed separately in Chapter 9. Even painting and sculpture are often hard to recognize in the traditional sense. In many contemporary works of art, such as constructions, assemblages, shaped canvases, and "environmental" art, painting and sculpture are so closely interrelated as to no longer exist as separate arts, one flat, the other three-dimensional.

The twentieth century has seen a dizzying progression of styles in the fine arts. A visitor from the Renaissance would find it unbelievable that a period no longer than a single life span could produce so many visions. In contrast to a unifying style which embraced every aspect of life in the past, from painting and architecture to jewelry and clothing, our visitor would encounter, to name only the most influential movements: fauvism, cubism, futurism, constructivism, dada, surrealism, and, most recently, abstract expressionism, pop art, op art, kinetic art, minimal art, junk art, funk art, psychedelic art, and happenings. Far from reflecting a unified view, these styles are remarkable for their range and extremes of contrast: from the cold geometry of minimal art to the strobe-lighted, mind-bending chaos of psychedelic art; from the hard brilliance of op to the soft organic forms of funk; and from the dribbled non-objective canvases of abstract expressionism to the flashy realism of pop.

The reproductions in this chapter survey the fine arts since World War II. They begin with two classic works of abstract expressionism, the first American movement to gain international renown, and include a few familiar and many less famous examples of other key movements.

Abstract Expressionism

Abstract expressionism represented an explosive break with the past. At their appearance in the mid 1940s, the bold, chaotic, and often carelessly painted canvases of the abstract expressionists aroused anger and confusion among critics and public. A violent rejection of subject matter and traditional painting methods, abstract expressionism discarded conscious planning and painstaking technique in favor of a highly emotional attack on the canvas. The result is a dynamic and tumultuous art of slashed, dripped, and splattered forms, which is, curiously, more expressive of our own time of psychological unease and riotous protest than of the relatively calm, business-as-usual years immediately following the war. For the artist — and his bewildered public — abstract expressionism was a painful break with the past which cleared the field for the multitude of art movements to follow.

Two important directions emerge in the examples of these movements illustrated and discussed on the following pages. They reflect two vital and related areas of contemporary culture: the technology of modern science and the media of communications, especially advertising. In the fine arts these points of view find expression in the paintings and three-dimensional constructions of op art and pop art.

Op Art

The eye-dazzling patterns of optical art are familiar to everyone. Op designs are not confined to the art gallery and museum but appear all around us: on brightly printed mini-dresses, ties, and shirts, on decorative wallpaper and wrapping paper, and even as jigsaw puzzles. Op art achieves its visually bewildering patterns by combining the bold shapes and flat colors of abstract art with the brilliant pigments of modern chemistry. The results are two effects of great fascination to contemporary artists: strong contrast and ambiguity. Although op art achieves these effects in a variety of ways, from simple black-and-white patterns to complicated constructions using ground lenses and reflective surfaces, there are three characteristics that most op works have in common: flat, toneless forms; uniform, over-all patterns — often rectangles, squares, and circles; and brilliant, high-contrast colors.

Op art reflects the experimentation of many artists with new developments in the science of optics. The op artist, whether working in two or three dimensions, uses color and pattern to manipulate our visual response. Some of the optical phenomena he explores are afterimages; the way the eye distinguishes between almost invisible differences in color, value, and shape; advancing and receding colors and shapes; and moiré patterns, which produce a vibrating effect. Some paintings are so subtle they require special lighting and sufficient time for the eye to adjust before differences in tone and shape emerge. Others are violent assaults so dazzling to the eye as to repel the viewer: these are related to the brilliant "consciousness-expanding" light-and-color effects of psychedelic art.

Pop Art

Of all the movements in the fine arts to have appeared in the last two decades, the most influential is undoubtedly pop art. In a sense, pop belongs to the oldest and most vigorous tradition in American art: the broad field of advertising. Before the advent of pop art, most artists drew a sharp line between "commercial" art and "fine" art. The former represented a hard-sell world of flashy billboards, slick magazine ads, packaging, and window displays, as well as the breathless fantasy of TV commercials, popular fiction, movie magazines, and comic strips, the rich material of America's popular culture. In the minds of most people nothing could be further from the serious world of the fine artist. Yet, in an odd way, the images and messages of popular culture display an energy and sense of purpose — and often a staggering vulgarity and ugliness — absent from much contemporary painting and sculpture.

Many people who are offended at finding comic strips, strawberry sundaes, and Brillo boxes in the art gallery are delighted to encounter them outside. In its natural state, pop art, in the form of communications media and consumer products, is meant to be taken very seriously indeed and does, in fact, stand at the center of our economy.

It is natural for us to expect art to be serious, to provide us with the experiences of order, beauty, and deep meaning that have always been hard to come by in life. Yet the pop artist is showing us that the things we make and buy and live with day in and day out are really quite extraordinary — if disquieting — and deserve the close examination and thoughtful attention usually reserved for loftier subjects. Perhaps, too, pop art is one way for the sensitive artist to deal with the confusion and shallow substance of the world that surrounds us. By isolating and enlarging the scale of soap boxes, paper bags, and movie heroines, the pop painter is able, as an artist, to triumph over a world that threatens to engulf him and all of us.

Many of the most compelling pop images are not those created by the trained artist in his studio but the "originals" found in the city, along the highway, and throughout our increasingly image-littered countryside in the form of billboards, gaudy "sculptures" beckoning us to motels and roadside fried chicken restaurants, store-window dummies, and plaster food displays. Pop art is not hard to find. The real difficulty lies in determining just what in our cluttered environment is *not* pop art.

Depending on one's sense of irony, the presence of pop — whether the work of a fine artist or the sales pitch of an untrained craftsman far removed from the sophisticated world of the art gallery — can be a satisfying or a frustrating experience. For many people, a six-foot paper bag is an affront to their intelligence and aesthetic sensibility, a body blow to everything they hold to be serious and valuable; for others, it is a clever — even brilliant — statement, which provides a sometimes painful but rewarding insight into the kind of world we live in.

Multi-media, Junk and Light

For those whose previous experience with art has been confined to traditional subjects such as landscape, portraits, figure paintings in oil and watercolor, and sculpture in marble and bronze, the examples of art in this chapter will come as a surprise — perhaps a shock. Not only has today's artist abandoned the images synonymous with art for centuries — which still seem familiar and valid to most people — he is exploring media and techniques for presenting his vision to the public unthought of a few years ago. Like the painters of the fifteenth century who revolutionized the vision and methods of their time with the newly developed oil medium, artists today are exploring the materials developed by modern chemistry and industry — synthetic media such as polymer, Magna, Lucite, lacquer, and fluorescent paints. The same revolution prevails in sculpture with welded metals and an endless array of soft and hard plastics. All these materials are brought together in that most complex form of fine art, the multi-media assemblage, which combines the materials of the painter and sculptor with the cast-off junk of our waste-producing society. Most significant for the future of art is the contemporary artist's use of light — neon, fluorescent tubes, and, in one instance reproduced here, pure beams of light aimed into the night sky, a fitting symbol of our devotion to eye-stunning contrasts and impermanence.

1
Woman I by Willem de Kooning. 1950-52. Oil on canvas. 75⅞ by 58 inches. (The Museum of Modern Art, New York. Purchase.)

2
Number 5 by Jackson Pollock. 1950. Oil on canvas. 53¾ by 39 inches. (The Museum of Modern Art, New York. Gift of Mr. and Mrs. Walter Bareiss.)

The two paintings on these pages, one nonobjective, the other an explosive figure, are landmarks in abstract expressionism. Bold, slashing brushstrokes and accidental effects mark the work of the turbulent movement that altered the course of painting in the decade following World War II.

3
Current by Bridget Riley. 1964. Polymer paint on composition board. 58⅜ by 58⅜ inches. (The Museum of Modern Art, New York. Philip C. Johnson Fund.)

The tightly spaced, undulating lines in Bridget Riley's famous op art painting seem to pull apart, then merge. To the eye of the observer, the result is optically exciting, pulsating waves of energy, like visible electric currents.

4
An unintentional op art pattern — the decorative printed liner from an airmail envelope.

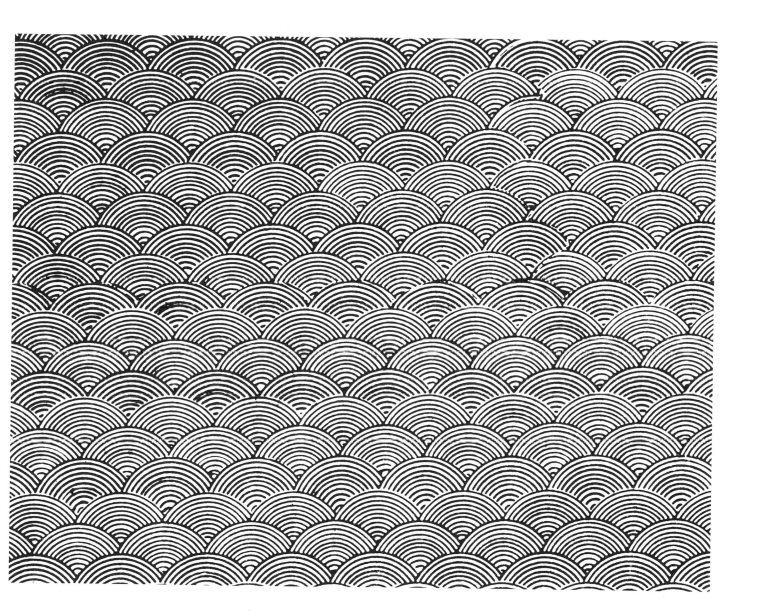

5

Equivocation by Ben Cunningham. 1964. Synthetic polymer paint on composition board. 26 by 26 inches. (The Museum of Modern Art, New York. Larry Aldrich Foundation Fund.)

One of the most widely reproduced op art paintings — recently used for a jigsaw puzzle. As the title suggests, Cunningham's geometric form, described by changes in the scale and direction of a checkerboard, is a visual "lie," designed to capture and hold the viewer by deceiving his eye.

6

Op art design from commercial gift-wrapping paper.

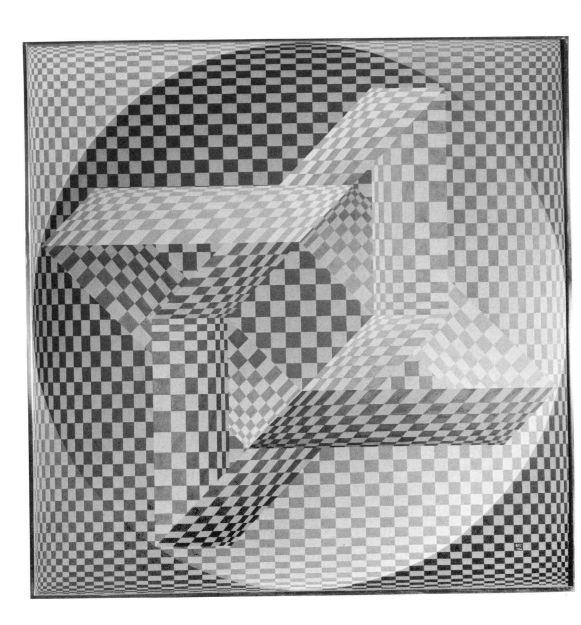

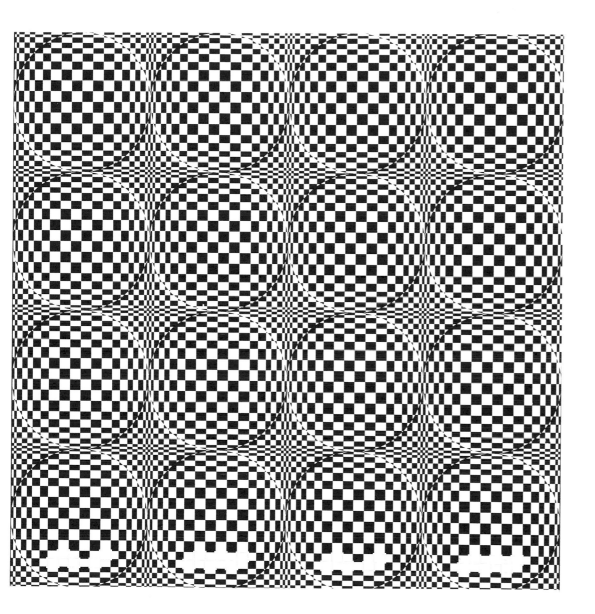

7
Matchbook covers magnified take on a bold and comic graphic quality. These simple advertisements, with their unsophisticated lettering and drawing and unconscious humor, have inspired such pop artists as Roy Lichtenstein, Andy Warhol, and James Rosenquist.

8

M-Maybe by Roy Lichtenstein. 1965. Oil and Magna on canvas. 60 by 60 inches. (Leo Castelli Gallery, New York. Photograph by Eric Pollitzer.)

To the pop artist, the breathless, life-and-death world of the comics — with its boldly outlined shapes and bright, flat colors — is a natural source for satire. What used to be regarded as trivial and vulgar entertainment for children and Sunday-supplement readers has, in the past few years, emerged as a field of serious study for sociologists, psychologists, and fine artists. Perhaps the classroom of the future will give equal time to Brenda Starr, Reporter and Lady Macbeth.

9

Time cover by Roy Lichtenstein. (Copyright 1968 Time Inc.)

The bold images on these pages illustrate a full cycle in the development of pop art. Inspired originally by the energetic and simple images of popular culture, pop, as a fine art, found its way into the galleries only to return to the vivid world of mass-circulation news coverage as a magazine cover.

10

Trade sign in the form of spectacles. Nineteenth century. Metal. 8 by 23 inches. (Milwaukee Art Center.)

Designed long before the advent of surrealism or pop art, this hypnotic sign is a marvelous example of both styles.

11

The Critic Sees 2 by Jasper Johns. 1964. Sculptmetal and glass, plaster core. 3¼ by 2⅛ inches. (Leo Castelli Gallery, New York. Collection of the artist.)

Open mouths emerge from the dark lenses of these eerie pop art spectacles.

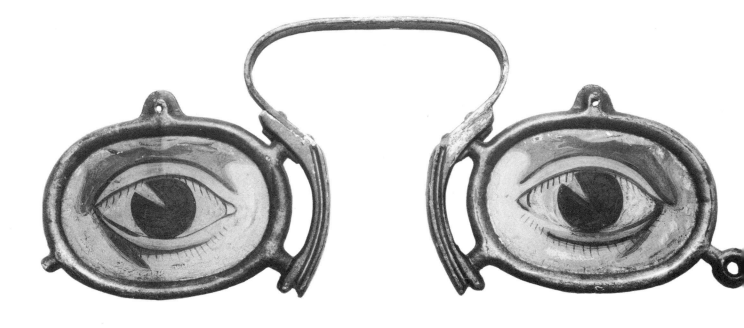

12

Odol by Stuart Davis.
1924. Oil on board. 24
by 18 inches. (The Down-
town Gallery, New York.
Photograph by Geoffrey
Clements.)

The vigorous graphic
images of American ad-
vertising affected the
vision of some painters as
early as the 1920s. *Odol*
is one of the first in-
stances of a fine artist
presenting a commercial
subject as a serious work
of art.

13

Brillo by Andy Warhol.
1964. Silk-screen ink on
wood. 17 by 17 by 14
inches. (Leo Castelli Gallery, New York. Photo-
graph by Rudolph
Burckhardt.)

An exact copy — in more
durable materials — of a
familiar supermarket item.

16
Mosaic pavement (detail) from The House of the Mysteries of Isis, Antioch, Roman. Early third century A.D. (The Art Museum, Princeton University.)

The optical illusion created by the reversible cube has intrigued artists for centuries. In Vasarely's painting, an op art version of this ancient pattern, attention is focused on the center of the design by gradually increasing the color intensity of the cubes.

15
Proton MC by Victor Vasarely. 1967. Oil on canvas. 65 by 65 inches. (Collection of Warner Le Roy, New York. Photo courtesy Sidney Janis Gallery, New York.)

33

17
The Gas Station by
George Segal. 1963. Mixed
media. 25 feet long.
(Courtesy Sidney Janis
Gallery, New York.)

In a dimly lighted gas
station, with its Coke machine, empty bottle rack,
oil cans, and tires, Segal's
figures, cast in plaster
from real people, show
the emotional detachment
of disaster victims.

18
Window display for Tex-
aco. A brilliant and dis-
turbing tableau, loaded
with symbols of our time:
gleaming plastic clothes,
glamourous machines,
and a case of high spirits
approaching madness.
(Photographs by Fortune
Monte.)

18a
Detail.

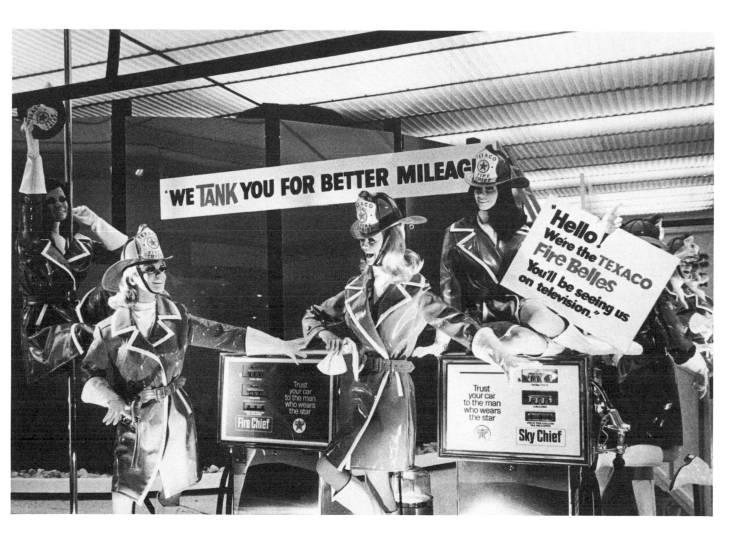

18
Paper Bag by Alex Hay.
1968. Painted paper,
epoxy, fiber glass. 22½
by 38 by 72 inches.
(Kornblee Gallery, New
York.)

19
Paper bag. (Courtesy L &
S Dairy Store, New York.)

Reproduced same size,
the two paper bags ap-
pear virtually identical.
In reality, however, the
"genuine" bag is about
fourteen inches high. The
artist's sculpture looms
six feet from the gallery
floor, a paper pop monu-
ment to gigantism and
the commonplace.

20
Giant shirt from store on
Fiftieth Street in New
York.

21
Giant Blue Shirt with Tie
by Claes Oldenburg. 1963.
Mixed media. 54 by 82
by 12 inches. (Courtesy
Sidney Janis Gallery,
New York.)

The gargantuan scale and
sagging weight of Olden-
burg's soft sculpture create a bizarre version of
the familiar business-
man's button-down shirt.

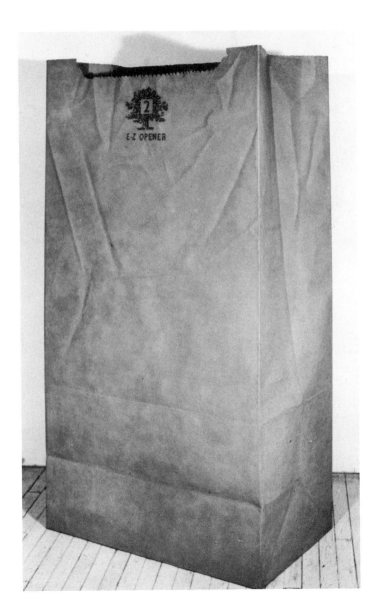

22 A & B
Two pop art sculptures from roadside America — the familiar yawning boy and a portly Southern gentleman — exhibit the curious lumpiness and cheerful vulgarity that lend such figures a poignant — but sometimes spooky — quality. (Photographs by Ron Carraher.)

23
Sun Bathers by Marisol. 1967. Mixed media. 89 by 38 by 40½ inches. (Courtesy Sidney Janis Gallery, New York. Photograph by Geoffrey Clements.)

Marisol brings sophistication and elegance to the flashy world of pop art. Reflecting sunlight onto their pale city faces, three figures convey the stylish aloofness of window dummies.

24
The Wait by Edward Kienholz. 1964-65. Mixed media. (Whitney Museum of American Art, New York. Gift of the Howard and Jean Lipman Fund. Photograph by Geoffrey Clements.)

Objects collected from life are combined in a ghoulish pop art environment. Bone-legged and cadaverous, wearing a grotesque necklace of bottled memories, a woman sits amidst domestic souvenirs: a caged bird, sewing basket, fringed floor lamp, and faded photos of her husband and children.

25
The human image survives in art, at least in these hand-painted ladies with their fashionable hairdos from a beauty parlor facade. (Photographs by Fortune Monte.)

26
Troy Donahue by Andy Warhol. 1964. Silk screen. A single head is about 10 inches high. (Leo Castelli Gallery, New York.)

Troy Donahue, a youth symbol of the fifties, is repeated in blurred, boring oval shapes, like faded Victorian locket photos. A pop art tribute to the bland, assembly-line good looks of the Hollywood film idol.

27
Advertisement for Corona beer in rural Puerto Rico. (Photograph by Harvey Schmidt.)

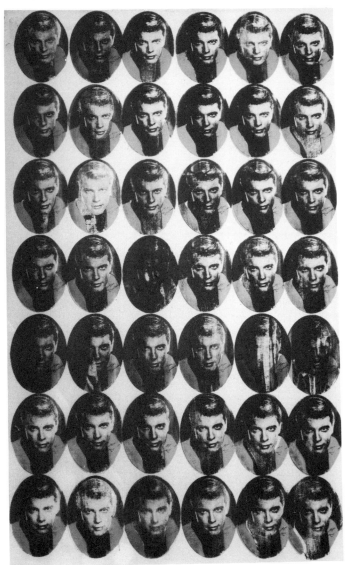

28
Hand-painted billboard for
Holsum bread. Surely one
of the most mysterious
images ever to flash past
the unwary motorist, it
projects as much uncon-
scious dread as any sur-
realist painting. (Foster
and Kleiser Company.)

29
Pies by Wayne Thiebaud.
1961. Oil. 22 by 28
inches. (Allan Stone
Gallery, New York.)

Food in all its forms, a
preoccupation of the affluent society, is a major
theme of pop art. These
tempting, creamy pies are
painted in oil using a full-
bodied, traditional impasto
technique.

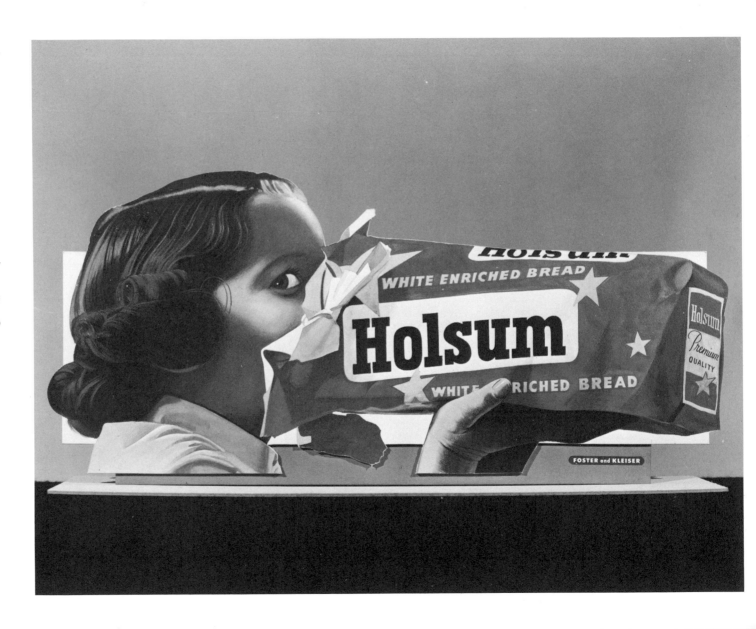

30
Automobile junk yard.
(N.Y. Daily News Photo.)

31
Butternut by John Chamberlain. 1963. Welded auto metal. 40 by 26 by 40 inches. (Collection Philippe Dotremont, Brussels. Photograph by Rudolph Burckhardt.)

Welded hunks of chrome and steel, the twisted remains of an automobile smash-up, reveal a surprising beauty of surface and form when they are isolated from the junk pile and placed on a pedestal.

32
Psychedelic car seen in New York's East Village. (Photograph by Fortune Monte.)

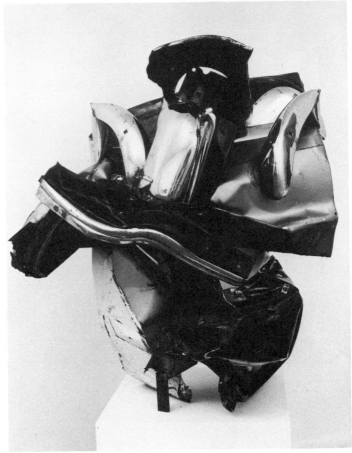

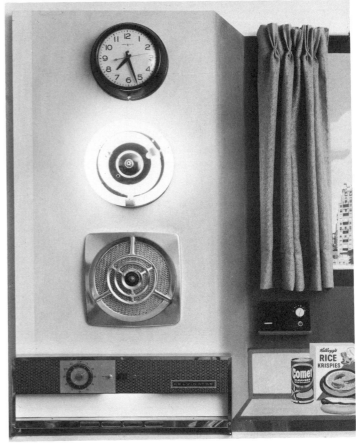

33
Study/Falling Man 1966
by Ernest Trova. Silicon
bronze. (Whitney Museum
of American Art, New
York. Photograph by
Geoffrey Clements.)

Decapitated and armless,
this chrome-smooth, chilling figure could symbol-
ize feelings of anxiety
and helplessness. Exhaust
pipes, grille, and wire
wheels add an uncom-
fortably sporty note.

34
Interior #1 by Tom Wes-
selmann. 1964. Real
clock, radio, light. 5 by 4
feet by 4 inches. (Collection Mr. and Mrs. Robert
C. Scull. Photograph by
Rudolph Burckhardt.)

In this pop art assem-
blage, the American
kitchen is seen as an
impersonal, mechanically
efficient "food prepara-
tion center." Wall clock,
fluorescent ring, air puri-
fier, automatic range, and
radio overwhelm the only
evidences of food — Rice
Krispies and a single hot
dog.

35
For the passerby casually
glancing into an empty
beauty parlor, electric hair
driers seem like ominous
and lonely machines for
survival in outer space.
(Photograph by Fortune
Monte.)

47

36
These anxious faces reflect the cosmetic perfection of the ideal modern family and — unwittingly — alienation and emptiness. (Photograph by Ron Carraher.)

37
The Beatles. Wax tableau. (The Museum of Famous People, New York.)

In the curious world of wax museums the deliberate effort to confuse art with life evokes an eerie, uncomfortable — but pleasurable — response, the aim of many pop artists.

38
Fried chicken being stabbed on a mammoth roadside billboard looms as food for giants and pop art in advertising for the motorist. (Foster and Kleiser.)

Foster and Kleiser

The family that prays together stays together
A FOSTER and KLEISER PUBLIC SERVICE MESSAGE

39
Gas by Allan Kaprow.
1966. (Photograph by
Peter Moore.)

40
Calling by Allan Kaprow.
1965. (Photograph by
Peter Moore.)

A synthesis of theater and
the visual arts, happen-
ings are a uniquely ap-
propriate art form for the
1960s. In these two ex-
amples — one takes place
in a surf covered with
foam, the other at the information booth in New
York's Grand Central Sta-
tion — the "actors" are
placed in absurd situa-
tions in "real-life" envi-
ronments. The result is
irrational, eerie — and
perversely comic.

41
Hagmatana III by Frank
Stella. 1967. Fluorescent
acrylic on canvas. 10 by
20 feet. (Leo Castelli Gallery, New York. Collection,
David Whitney. Photograph
by Rudolph Burckhardt.)

Stella's rainbow-hued,
hard-edge geometric de-
signs combine lively en-
ergy with an almost
architectural scale.

43
Instability Through Movement by Julio le Parc. 1962-64. Construction of painted wood and aluminum. 28⅝ by 57⅛ by 26½ inches. (The Museum of Modern Art, New York. Inter-American Fund.)

Movement — by the spectator rather than the work of art — is the most important element of Le Parc's sculpture. The reflective aluminum sheets seem to bulge and warp when viewed from different angles, like terrified eyes reacting to sharp changes of light.

44
Hatching Egg by Jean Tinguely. 1958. Motorized construction of painted metal and plywood. 30½ by 32½ by 9 inches. (The Museum of Modern Art, New York. Gift of Erwin Burghard Steiner.)

Time and space are the most compelling facts of life today — the exploration of outer space and the population explosion their most immediate manifestations. With kinetic sculpture, the artist shows us that nothing stands still in time — relationships are in constant flux.

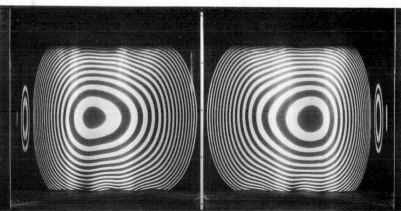

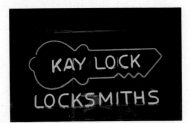

KAY LOCK
LOCKSMITHS

WORLD'S
BEST
COFFEE

NN ARCADE
THRU TO 33rd ST.

CHINESE VILLAGE
CHOP SUEY
ENTRANCE IN ARCADE

flowers

BARBER
SHOP

FRED GRUMAN'S
SKATE SHOP INC.

EXPERT
Tailoring

BAR

44

Center: *Fragments for the Gates to Times Square II* by Chryssa. 1966. Neon and plexiglass. 43 by 34$\frac{1}{16}$ by 27$\frac{1}{16}$ inches. (Pace Gallery, New York.)

Left and right: Neon street signs. (Photographs by Harvey Schmidt.)

A gateway from the fine arts and commercial signs present contrasting visions of modern neon art and design. Chryssa's angular, brilliant sculpture is a creative symbol. The neon signs invite the viewer to a wide variety of commercial functions, from locksmith to bar.

45

Albuquerque by Stanley Landsman. 1968. From the exhibition "Light: Object & Image." (Whitney Museum of American Art, New York. Photograph by Geoffrey Clements.)

Light and reflective surfaces are the newest and most stunning media to be explored by the contemporary artist.

SCULPTURE IN
ENVIRONMENT

For six weeks in 1967 —
from October 1 to November 15 — the New York
City Department of
Recreation and Cultural
Affairs sponsored a remarkable art exhibition.
From Harlem to the Battery, Manhattan burst
forth with giant indoor
and outdoor sculptures by
twenty-four of the nation's
leading artists. Considering the timidity — or outright distrust — with
which most city offices
regard art in any of its
many forms, this show
was particularly heartening. Some of the sculptures, besides being — to
put it mildly — larger
than life, belonged to the
class of art known as
"miminal" and "brutal" —
looming geometric shapes
like giant fragments
hurled to earth from
outer space. For the six
weeks they were on display, New Yorkers of all
ages and stations — from
ghetto children to Park
Avenue executives — were
variously shocked, intrigued, amazed, and delighted by them.

The ten sculptures reproduced on pages 54 to 59
include works in sheet
steel, plywood, clear plastics, and, in one instance,
powerful beams of light
aimed at the sky and visible at night for several
miles. Some are so geometrically perfect as to
repel any advance by the
passer-by; others invite
him to touch or actually
walk through them. One
shows the brilliant light
effects the artist can
achieve with neon — a
medium used with inventive genius in advertising
art for decades. All of the
sculptures evidence the
daring efforts of some of
today's artists to deal with
the difficult problem of
creating monumental
three-dimensional forms
for public display. (Photographs 46-55 by Fred W.
McDarrah.)

46
Offering and *Alpha* by
Alexander Lieberman.
Battery Park.

47
All Star Cast by Les Le-
vine. 1967. America's
Plaza, Time-Life Building.

48
Boss Linco by Lyman Kipp. 1967. Mall, Central Park.

49
Alamo by Bernard Rosenthal. Astor Place.

50
The Broken Obelisk by Barnett Newman. 1963-67. Seagram Building Plaza.

51
Orange Vertical Floor Neon by Stephen Antonakos. 1967. New York University Loeb Student Center.

52
Cuboid Shift #2 by Paul Frazier. City Hall.

53
Diamond by Antoni Milkowski. Kips Bay Plaza.

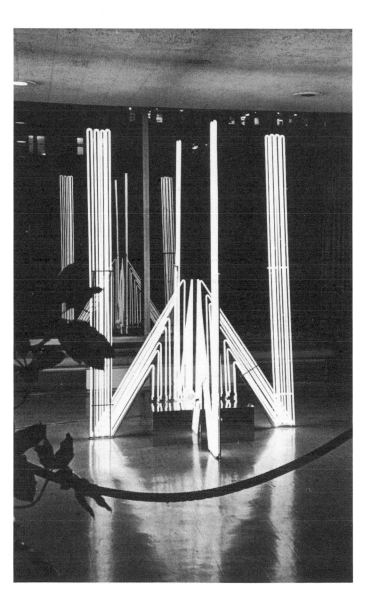

54
Untitled Sculpture by Bernard Kirschenbaum. 1967.
Terrace overlooking Bethesda Fountain.

55
Searchin by Forrest Meyers. Projected from Tompkins Square Park.

4. Shapes of Our Time

A favorite parlor game of the twentieth century is to imagine what odd fragments of our civilization might endure through hundreds of years to greet the puzzled eyes of a future archaeologist. Would the relics of our world be as beautiful and moving as the sculpture, furniture, and painting discovered in Egypt in the ancient tombs of the Pharoahs? Probably not. Unlike the Egyptians we do not place our most valued possessions in tombs to accompany the occupants into the afterlife. Except for objects unearthed in tomb burials, most archaeological finds are merely scattered bits and pieces — broken vases, fragments of sculpture, combs, coins, weapons of war — poignant reminders of man's greatness and smallness and, most of all, his mortality.

Unfortunately for his historical image, man is seldom able to arrange in advance which artifacts of his time and place will end up in museum showcases. Added to this uncertainty is the unhappy tendency in our own time of instant change to tear down our monuments almost as fast as we put them up. In just a little over fifty years, Pennsylvania Station, one of New York City's great landmarks, passed from an imposing monument to — during its demolition in 1964 — an archaeological ruin, to become, finally, a fading memory.

If we were suddenly to suffer a natural disaster like the volcanic eruption that buried — and preserved intact — the ancient Roman city of Pompeii in 79 A.D. or, as many people realistically fear, a man-made nuclear holocaust, it would be a small comfort at least to know that we were leaving behind as evidence of our style and ingenuity San Francisco's Golden Gate Bridge rather than a drive-in nutburger stand, even though each, in its own way, would tell a lot about us.

Rather than wait for disasters, natural or man-made,

a number of artifacts, most of them products of the last ten years, have been selected to offer the designer and student of the future a capsule glimpse of a few of the objects that have special meaning to our time. With a couple of exceptions the designs on the following pages are the inventions of pure science and engineering, the shapes of an age of technology. Unlike the constructions of the contemporary sculptor, they were not designed to be works of art. Curiously enough, however, many of the forms reproduced here, notably the hardware of space exploration and supersonic jet aircraft, are of a remarkably high aesthetic caliber, often surpassing in energy and vitality works produced by the artist in his studio. Although all of the objects illustrated are "useful," their significance varies dramatically — from the familiar Coke bottle to the F-111 jet fighter. In one way or another, however, these forms constitute a small but dynamic index of our time.

1
Microminiaturized switching unit from a computer. The unit, shown here greatly enlarged, is about one inch long. The rhythmic geometric pattern bears a surprising resemblance to a contemporary hard-edge abstract painting. (Photograph by Henry Groskinsky, LIFE Magazine. Copyright Time Inc.)

TK-42 Color Television
Camera. (RCA.)

3
Panasonic model CT-61P, portable color television set. TV is probably the most powerful force at work in the world today and for most people the hardest thing — after food and drink — to do without. This Panasonic is a classic example of compact design — a rare combination of elegance and usefulness.

4
Farberware toaster no. 271.

5
IBM System 360. This clean-cut shape, which disguises the extraordinarily complex inner workings of data-processing equipment, is among the most compelling and frequently repeated forms of our time. Anyone unfamiliar with our technological culture would find it difficult to tell if he were confronting an IBM system, automatic range, washer-dryer, refrigerator, or stereo console.

Four products of modern technology — ranging in function from a sober IBM computer to a pop-up toaster — share the clean, angular stamp of aerodynamic design.

63

6
Six U.S. Air Force swing-wing F-111A fighter-bombers. (U.S. Air Force.)

7
Boeing SST supersonic jet transport (mock-up). The multiple exposure photograph shows how the wings will be extended for takeoff and landing. When it goes into service, the SST will carry as many as 350 passengers at a speed of 1,800 miles an hour. (The Boeing Company.)

8
Four-level cloverleaf in
Los Angeles, a graceful
pattern dictated by the
complex and heavy auto-
mobile traffic of a far-
flung modern city.

9
Nuclear bomb, bearing
the disarmingly innocent
nickname "Little Boy."
The kind of bomb deto-
nated over Hiroshima in
World War II, it is 28
inches in diameter and 120
inches long. It weighed
9,000 pounds and had a
yield equivalent to about
20,000 tons of high ex-
plosive, quite modest by
today's standards. (Los
Alamos Scientific Lab-
oratory.)

Flight through space and
high-speed travel on the
ground have produced
the most powerful and
dynamic forms of our time.

10
Italian folding chair. Ca. 1500. Walnut with inlaid work of ivory and metal. (The Metropolitan Museum of Art. Gift of William H. Riggs, 1913.)

11
"Vienna" café chair by Gebruder Thonet. 1876. Bent beechwood. (The Museum of Modern Art, New York. Purchase.)

12
Lounge chair (Barcelona chair) by Ludwig Mies Van Der Rohe. 1929. Chrome-plated steel bars and leather. (The Museum of Modern Art, New York. Gift of the manufacturer: Knoll Associates, Inc.)

13
Dining chair by Charles Eames. 1946. Molded walnut plywood and metal rod. (The Museum of Modern Art, New York. Gift of the manufacturer: Herman Miller Furniture Co., U.S.A.)

14
Chair by Gunnar Aagaard Anderson. 1966. Urethane foam. (The Museum of Modern Art, New York. Gift of the designer.)

The chair — an inanimate extension of the human body — can reveal a great deal about the time for which it was made. Each of the five examples shown here represents the most advanced furniture design of its time.

One of the most beautiful designs in the history of furniture, the exquisitely inlaid Renaissance chair could be folded up and carried into battle to provide an instant throne of command for a general.

The famous café chair is the best known of several graceful bentwood pieces designed by the German Michael Thonet. Chairs based on Thonet's original design can still be seen in restaurants all over the world.

The chrome and leather Barcelona chair, designed almost forty years ago by Ludwig Mies Van Der Rohe, remains today, like many designs of the prolific and daring 1920s, a high-water mark of modern refinement and elegance.

The most famous furniture design to appear since World War II (and possibly in this century), the Eames chair clearly reflects an age of aerodynamics in its minimal use of materials and airy lightness. Curiously, it bears a strong likeness to some of the hardware developed to explore the moon's surface.

Typical of much art in the 1960s is an open delight in the perverse, a flouting of conventional functions and forms. An updated version of the old-fashioned overstuffed chair, symbol of domestic comfort and security, Anderson's great oozing lump of urethane plastic looks like a sloppily iced chocolate cake.

15
Coca-Cola 6½-ounce bot-
tle. One of the most dur-
able and satisfying shapes
of the twentieth century
(slightly obscured here by
beads of sweat calculated
to excite your thirst). (The
Coca-Cola Company.)

16
The evolution of the Coca-
Cola fountain glass from
the earlier tapered shape
to the current rounded
glass. (The Coca-Cola
Company. Photograph by
Harold J. Terhune.)

17
Greyhound's experimental
MC-6X cross-country bus.
(Greyhound Corporation.)

18
The Necchi 544 sewing
machine combines precise
function with an aesthet-
ically pleasing organic
form probably influenced
by contemporary abstract
sculpture. (Necchi S.p.
A., Pavia, Italy.)

19
Olivetti Lettera 22. A distinguished product of modern mass production, this typewriter has the compact elegance and energetic detail of fine sculpture. (Olivetti Underwood Corporation.)

20
Vespa motorscooter. As elegant as it is practical, the Vespa revolutionized transportation in postwar Italy.

21
Parker "51" Standard Pen. As streamlined as a torpedo.

The hardware of space
exploration represents the
most advanced technology
of the twentieth century.
These amazing space-
craft — perfect expression
of the idea "form follows
function" — are, in some
instances, more reminis-
cent of old-fashioned ceil-
ing fans or the internal
workings of washing ma-
chines than the glamour-
ous aerodynamic forms
envisioned for decades by
the comics for the ex-
ploration of outer space.
Others, like Essa I, have
a subtle geometric beauty
quite as pleasing as con-
temporary sculpture cre-
ated by the artist in his
studio.

22
Essa I satellite. Cameras
aboard take cloud pictures
and transmit them to
ground stations. (RCA
Astro-electronics Div.)

23
Lunar Orbiter (model).
The spacecraft's function
is to orbit the moon
and take close-up photos
of the lunar surface. The
four black paddles are
solar panels; the two
white arms are antennas.
(The Boeing Company.)

24
Surveyor I (model) was designed to examine possible astronaut landing sites on the moon. (JPL/NASA.)

25
Test model of the Apollo lunar excursion module (LEM). It weighs about 2,600 pounds and is nineteen feet high and twenty feet wide. (NASA.)

26
Saturn V rocket with its Apollo spacecraft payload. The 364-foot Saturn V/Apollo, shown here mounted on a crawler, was designed for a manned landing on the moon. (The Boeing Company.)

27
Unidentified flying object photographed in Zanesville, Ohio, November 13, 1966. Flying saucers are the most controversial and mysterious forms of our time. If they are indeed visitors from an alien planet they could determine the future of our world. If they are not from outer space (nor the result of "marsh gas" as some experts have offered) they may represent the most universal hallucination in history. (Wide World Photos.)

5. Minimal Art — the "Clean, Uncluttered" Form

Beginning in the 1960s, visitors to museums and art galleries were confronted with an astonishing — and to most people, perplexing — new style: minimal art. Even sophisticated lovers of art who are familiar with the dozens of new movements that have occurred during the past twenty-five or thirty years are taken aback when faced with the spectacle of a six-foot metal cube looming before their eyes in a quiet sculpture garden or a large unframed black square sharing wall space with traditional still-life and landscape paintings. Unlike even the most abstract or nonobjective art, which though it may abandon recognizable subject matter usually bears a strong trace of the sculptor's or painter's touch, the new minimal forms betray absolutely no trace of the artist's hand. As the sculptures and paintings on the following pages indicate, they look like the coldly perfect, machine-made products of mass production. Instead of the subtly modeled surfaces and rich textures typical of most traditional sculpture, whether abstract or representational, minimal forms — cubes, rectangles, slabs, circles, and three-dimensional geometric grids — delight in the faultlessly smooth surfaces we associate with automobiles and kitchen appliances.

Minimal art is also called primary structure, ABC art, and reductive art. All of these terms — whether we are talking about sculpture and painting or the products of modern industry — suggest certain characteristics. Chief among these is bold geometric form. In the long and complex history of art and design few man-made forms are so stark in outline and so utterly shorn of surface embellishment. Many of the materials of the minimal artist are synthetic products of modern chemistry, notable for their uniform, mechanical surfaces: acrylic and lacquer paints, fiber glass, urethane foam, Lucite, Dacron, vinyl, formica, and epoxy. Other media are associated with industry or advertising: stainless steel, chrome, aluminum, vacuum-plated glass, fluorescent and neon lights — materials that recognize our contemporary fascination with highly reflective surfaces and transparency.

Minimal paintings are even more stark in design. At their extreme they are so reduced as to be no more than monochromatic squares, rectangles, or circles — ideal geometric shapes that prevent any deep emotional involvement on the part of the spectator. The experience of attending an exhibition of minimal painting can result in embarrassing and comic situations: After viewing a number of unadorned painted rectangles and smooth-surfaced slabs, gallery visitors have found themselves staring attentively at a similar object, seemingly a part of the show, only to discover after a minute or two of serious study that it is a closed door leading to another room or the metal covering of the gallery's electrical fuse box.

However confusing and exasperating it may sometimes be when it is encountered in the fine arts, minimal form is not the concern of just the avant-garde painter and sculptor. It is a major force in contemporary design that pops up wherever we look: in clothes (throw-away paper dresses, the mini-skirt), in look-alike office skyscrapers built from the same mass-produced modular units, and in sleek cubistic household appliances — refrigerators, stoves, dishwashers, TV sets, toasters — all, regardless of their widely differing functions, forced into the same smooth, geometric form and bearing a strong family resemblance to that most severe of all modern minimal shapes: the computer.

Once the eye becomes alerted to minimal form, we

find it everywhere in contemporary life. As we wait for an elevator we notice that the closed white doors, forming a thin dark line where they meet, resemble a Barnett Newman abstract painting; the nearby elevator control box, a severely plain metal square, is the double for an early Rauschenberg unpainted canvas; a fluorescent lighting fixture is the twin of a Flavin light sculpture.

For decades, educators and designers have championed the idea of "clean, uncluttered" form in the design of all objects, from industrial mass production to one-of-a-kind crafts. At its extreme, this concept abhors any manipulation of form or surface embellishment that disguises the true function of an object. A dinner plate, for example, is seen merely as a circular support for food; any added flight of fancy, such as a floral pattern (or, as in the more dramatic case of fifteenth-century Renaissance platters, of royal portraits or scenes from the Greek myths) is frowned upon as a violation of the plate's purely mechanical function.

In part this attitude stems from the justifiable reaction among conscientious designers to the practice in the nineteenth century, during the early years of machine technology, of attempting to invest products of the assembly line with the made-by-hand elegance of traditional crafts. So strong was the reaction against what many considered an unfeeling use of design to mask the real functions of the new inventions (sewing machines enmeshed in cast-iron blooms and vines, plumbing fixtures patterned after rococo palace furniture) that the very word "decorative" is used today by many designers to imply weakness, sentimentality, and lack of importance.

This philosophy leads inevitably to objects of great purity of form and, finally, to minimal form. As some of the examples here and in Chapter 4 illustrate, it is capable of producing objects that are arresting and satisfying. This is particularly true in those instances when industry has tapped the talents of sensitive designers who are able to meet the strict demands of machine production and still invest their work with great beauty of form, as in the Olivetti Lettera 22 typewriter (page 69), or the one-of-a-kind trademark sculpture designed for ABC (page 84).

The same philosophy applied to painting can reach a dead end. As art objects, the square, the rectangle, and their variations can quickly exhaust our powers of emotional and intellectual involvement. To put it bluntly: they are likely to bore us. As in all art forms, including movies, TV, or music, when there is little or no variation or contrast, the mind ceases to be concerned with the "message" and turns elsewhere for meaning and stimulation.

A famous painter of minimal works of art has stated that his spare forms signal the death of painting, a point beyond which the artist ceases to function. Many people who are deeply concerned with art feel that this is probably true. Two-dimensional works of art — canvases and panels designed to be hung on the wall and observed from a fixed point of view — are rapidly giving way to constructions in space, which combine color with three dimensions. With its chilling geometric shapes and uniform surfaces, minimal form symbolizes two strong tendencies of our times: our rejection of the human form in art and design and our embracing of the technology of modern science.

1
The Wild by Barnett Newman. 1950. Oil on canvas. 95¾ by 1⅝ inches. (On extended loan to The Museum of Modern Art, New York, from The Kulicke Foundation.)

2
Elevator door in a modern Park Avenue office skyscraper. (Photograph by Fortune Monte.)

3
Inlaid elevator door from the Chrysler Building in New York City. (Photograph by Fortune Monte.)

Barnett Newman's spare painting, like a strip of adhesive tape, and the elevator door (2) reflect our contemporary concern with minimal form on two different levels: fine art and interior design. The elevator door from the Chrysler Building was designed in 1929. A surprisingly short span of time separates it from today's bare surfaces.

4
Buffet plate by Arabia of Finland. (Courtesy Georg Jensen.)

5
Decorated Italian majolica plate. 1515-1525. (The Metropolitan Museum of Art, Gift of V. Everit Macy, 1927, in memory of his wife, Edith Carpenter Macy.)

6
Advertisement for 1903 model refrigerator. (The Bettmann Archive.)

7
Refrigerator-freezer. (Frigidaire Division of General Motors Corporation.)

8
Hotpoint automatic washer.

9
Roller washing machine 1865. (The Bettmann Archive.)

Household appliances in their infancy show markedly different forms. The modern versions of the refrigerator and washer are first cousins, sharing the same minimal styling: solid rectangular form and sleek white enamel finish.

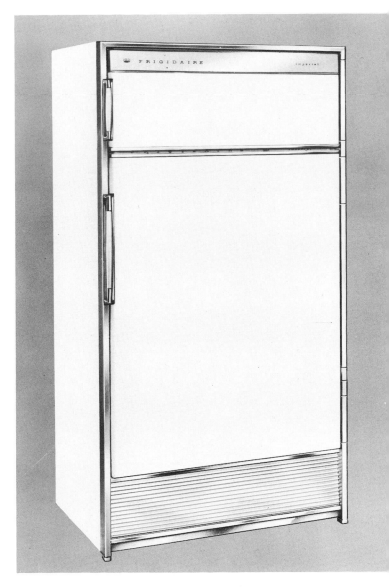

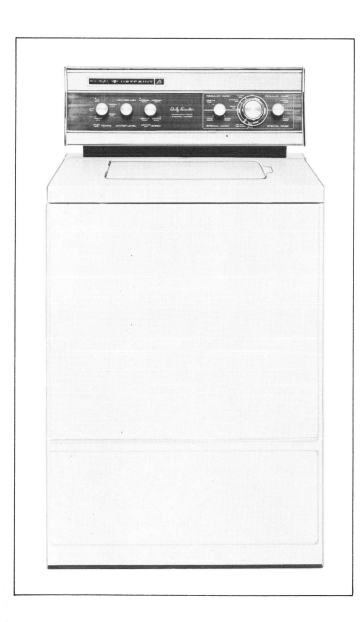

10
SDS Sigma 5 computer.
(Scientific Data System.)

11
White Painting by Robert
Rauschenberg. 1951-68.
House paint on canvas. 72
by 126 inches (seven
units). (Leo Castelli Gallery, New York. Collection
the artist.)

12
Interior screen wall from
a modern office building.

Three minimal forms com-
posed of modular panels
represent widely contrasting design areas: com-
puter technology, contem-
porary painting, and
interior design. The
Rauschenberg painting
and the panel wall are
identical twins. They present an uncanny coinci-
dence of design solutions,
one from the artist's studio, the other from the engineer's drawing board.

13
Thousands (detail) by Bill Komodore. 1964. Synthetic polymer paint on canvas. 60½ by 49½ inches. (Whitney Museum of American Art, New York. Photograph by Geoffrey Clements.)

14
Detail of the facade of a modern office building showing use of modular window units. (Photograph by Fortune Monte.)

15
Model of New York City's World Trade Center, designed by Yamasaki. (Wide World Photos.)

16
Electro-Spectral Group No. 1 by Boyd Mefford. 1967. (Whitney Museum of American Art, New York. Lent by Milwaukee Art Center and Nancy Singer Gallery. Photograph by Geoffrey Clements.)

The world's tallest skyscrapers and a contemporary sculpture incorporating bands of colored light share the same vertical minimal form.

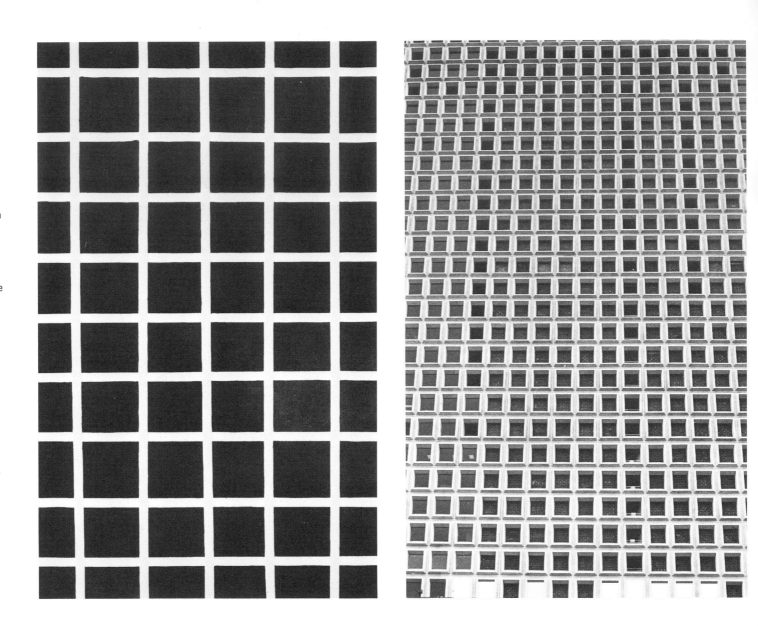

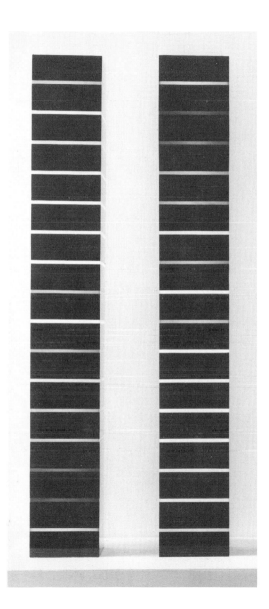

17
Fluorescent lighting ring in a subway-concourse bakery. (Photograph by Fortune Monte.)

18
Untitled sculpture by Dan Flavin. 1966. Fluorescent lights. (Whitney Museum of American Art. Gift of the Howard and Jean Lipman Fund. Photograph by Geoffrey Clements.)

19
Child's table and nesting stool by Riki Watanabe. Die-cut corrugated cardboard. (Museum of Contemporary Crafts, from "Made with Paper.")

20
Paper mini-dress. (Courtesy Gail Siegel.)

Minimal forms from the environment and from the designer, using two familiar materials: glass and paper.

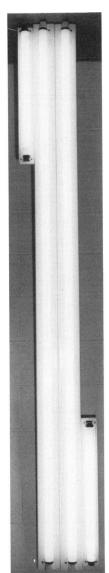

21
New York Telephone
Company building. This
severely geometric, win-
dowless sculpture looms
over Manhattan's West
Side like a huge minimal
sculpture. (New York
Telephone Company.)

22
Metal door of an elevator
control box. (Photograph
by Fortune Monte.)

23
Abstract Painting by Ad
Reinhardt. 1960-61. Oil on
canvas. 60 by 60 inches.
(The Museum of Modern
Art, New York. Purchase.)

24
American Broadcasting Company trademark sculpture. (Photograph by Fortune Monte.)

25
Description of Table by Richard Artschwager. 1964. Formica. 26¼ by 32 by 32 inches. (Whitney Museum of American Art. Gift of the Howard and Jean Lipman Foundation, Inc. Photograph by Geoffrey Clements.)

26
Die II by Tony Smith. 1967. Steel. 6 by 6 by 6 feet. (Fischbach Gallery, New York.)

27
Untitled sculpture (detail) by Larry Bell. 1966. Glass and metal. 12¼ by 12¼ by 12¼ inches. (Pace Gallery, New York. Photograph by Ferdinand Boesch.)

Four variations on the theme of the cube, employing such diverse media as glass, steel, plastic, and concrete.

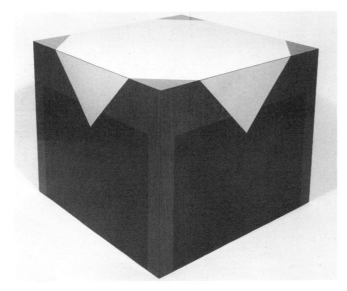

Since its birth in the late nineteenth century, the automobile has become, along with the telephone and — most recently — the television, one of the determining inventions of modern times. The automobile industry, together with the sectors it largely supports — steel, petroleum, and highway construction — is the richest and most powerful business in the world. The car has dramatically altered the lives of everyone in our technological society; it is also a symbol of profound personal meaning. For the adult, the family car is the prime contact with an increasingly mobile world, from short hauls to the shopping center — itself an outgrowth of the car — to vacations encompassing thousands of miles. For the teen-ager, the use of the automobile signals the arrival of his independence, a break with the family, a life of his own mounted on wheels. To a large extent the modern city, and especially its sprawling suburbs, is a product of the car. Almost every function important to modern life can be performed from behind the steering wheel. We can shop from the car, bank, go to the movies, eat dinner, and, in automotively advanced areas, particularly the West Coast, even worship and attend funerals from the isolated comfort of the front seat.

Although many people still living today can recall the sight of an early automobile spluttering down a quiet village street, the history of the car is surprisingly long. For centuries man dreamed of a "horseless carriage." As long ago as the sixteenth century, Leonardo da Vinci conceived of a self-powered vehicle. However, not until the beginnings of industrial technology in the late eighteenth century was a practical source of power — the steam engine — developed which could propel a heavy machine with human passengers.

The earliest predecessor of the automobile was invented in 1769 by the Frenchman Nicolas Cugnot. It was a huge tricycle powered by steam and it propelled four passengers at a sedate two and a quarter miles per hour. This awkward and enormous machine must have presented an alarming spectacle as it inched ponderously through the French countryside. From Cugnot's steam-powered tricycle to today's precision-engineered, gasoline-engine automobile with its self-adjusting seats, air-conditioning, and eight-track stereo set represents a breathtaking advance in the style of personal transportation.

Although the first American gasoline-powered car, the invention of Charles Duryea, appeared as early as 1892, the most sophisticated early gasoline-powered automobiles are credited to the Germans Carl Benz (in 1885) and Gottlieb Daimler (in 1886). Henry Ford is popularly thought of as the father of the auto assembly line; however, the first mass-produced car in the United States was the 1902 Oldsmobile. Ford's greatest contribution to the early growth of the automobile was the development of a car cheap enough to be bought by the masses — a revolutionary step that changed the pattern of life in Europe and America.

The capsule history of the Ford illustrated on pages 88 and 89 traces the evolution of that car from 1896 to 1968. In its early years the automobile clearly showed its origins. The first models looked exactly like small carriages with the horse missing. Like the first telephones, illustrated in Chapter 2, the earliest cars were functional machines, products of the mechanical engineer, not the stylist. By the 1920s, however, the car had assumed the general form it was to maintain: a compact box on wheels with an engine in front and with an en-

Detail of Bentley. (Photograph by Alexandre Georges.)

closed passenger area. By 1925, the automobile had entered its great classic period, which lasted for about fifteen years, to the outbreak of World War II. This was the era of the beautiful custom-built luxury cars that combined high speeds (up to 130 miles per hour) with comparable prices (as much as $40,000). These are the automobiles with aristocratic names that fascinate car buffs today. Among the most famous are Rolls-Royce, Hispano-Suiza, Bugatti, Talbot, Duesenberg, Mercedes-Benz, and Isotta-Fraschini. In America, classic models reached a high point in the late 1930s and in 1940 with the appearance of the Cadillac 60 Special and the Lincoln Continental. These two cars are classics because their elegant forms express perfectly the special function of the car as a fast-moving vehicle of private transportation. Their subtly curving, sharp-edged planes and refined details relate them equally to the science of engineering and the art of sculpture.

After the war, the newly revived automobile industry felt the impact of two conflicting approaches to design. The first appeared in the sleek, unadorned cars coming from Italy, most notably those from the design studios of Pinin Farina in Turin. The avant-garde Italian styles exercised a deep influence on the design of sports cars — and some stock models — all over the world. In sharp contrast were the bizarre designs of the automobiles which rolled off the assembly lines in Detroit during the 1950s. These flashy postwar models signaled the end of classic car design and the arrival of the full baroque period of the American car. Automobile design fell under the compelling influence of the jet plane: the chassis puffed out and burst forth with a wild array of embellishments — fins, "jet-away" taillights, gaudy chrome "flight" strips, stabilizers, and air scoops. Zap-

ping along the thruway, the family car looked like a wayward pop-art assemblage from outer space.

By 1960, aerodynamic fantasy in car design had reached its peak. The first American compacts were introduced (Chevrolet's Corvair, Ford's Falcon, and Chrysler's Valiant) in an attempt to stem the rising tide of small foreign imports. In general, however, cars of the 1960s have been characterized by an increase in size. While the showy ornamentation of the previous decade has been on the wane, the automobile stylist still identifies his product with the age of flight. A recent TV commercial cheerfully described a new model as the car "with a cockpit that looks like it belongs on a supersonic jet."

To the distress of advocates of automotive safety, the automobile industry in recent years has pursued a policy of naming its products after animals known for speed or ferocity. Gone are such bland designations as Ford, Plymouth, and Dodge; today's thrill-seeking driver is offered instead: Mustang, Barracuda, Falcon, Stingray, Wildcat, and Cougar, as well as the less specific but equally evocative Fury, Marauder, Javelin, Charger, Tempest, and Rebel.

While cars of the future are not likely to lose their aggressive image, built-in safety is an increasing concern to drivers and manufacturers alike. There is also talk of other sources of power such as electricity and even steam, which would help to control the mounting problem of air pollution. In all the current change and speculation, one thing is clear: the automobile will continue to appeal as much to our sense of fantasy and art as it will to our need for a practical way to get about in the world.

This series of photographs on pages 88 and 89 traces the design development of the Ford from 1896 to the present day. As in the evolution of the telephone, the design of the automobile has undergone a fascinating change during the course of its annual "face-lifting." What begins as a crude-looking, slow-moving horseless carriage becomes a design classic during the 1920s and the early thirties. Later models reflect the impact of the jet age, with aerodynamically designed chassis and such jet-inspired details as tail fins, hooded headlights, and massive taillights.

1
1896. The first Ford was a motorized version of the carriage of its time. Both engine and passengers were exposed to the weather. The driver steered with a tiller.

2
1903. Model A. The engine is partially concealed; a steering wheel has replaced the tiller. Lamps make driving at night possible.

3
1909. Model N. The engine is completely covered and moved forward. The addition of a roof and rear doors gives the passengers some protection. The automobile begins to assume a "normal" appearance.

4
1922. Model T. Completely enclosed doors and glass windows permit all-weather driving in this touring car.

5
1923. Model T station wagon. Roll-up curtains add a jaunty note to this prototype of today's popular wagon.

6
1929. Model A. By the late 1920s the automobile loses its angular, "archaic" shape to assume a more rounded, sculptural form.

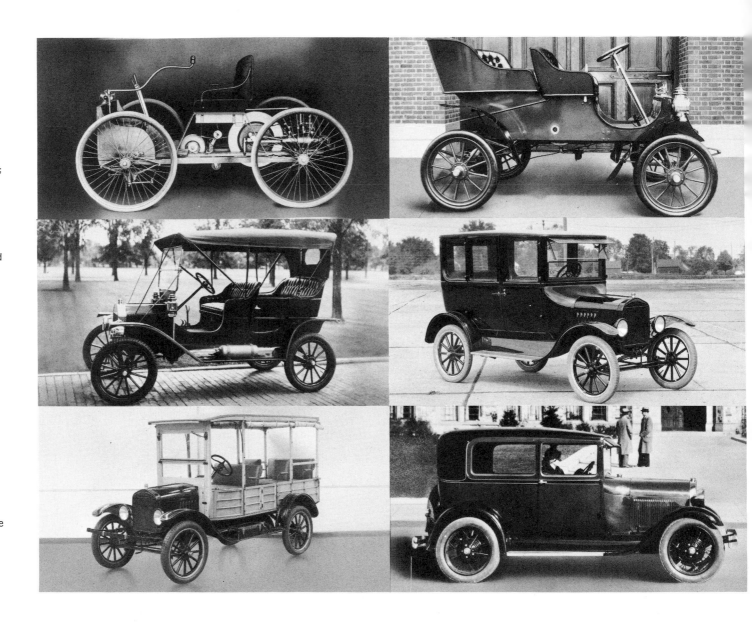

7
1934. V-8. Further refinement of the flowing contour.

8
1936. V-8. A sporty-looking two-passenger coupe. The sensitive lines and harmonious detailing lend this model a classical feeling.

9
1941. V-8. Four-passenger coupe. A further simplification in design results in a bulkier chassis with minimal running board and headlights incorporated into the body.

10
1949. First major postwar model change. The tendency, seen in the 1941 model, to incorporate details in the body is carried further here by making fenders part of the total chassis design.

11
1957. The Fairlane reflects the flashy look of the fifties with its emphasis on jet styling in side metal decoration, huge hooded headlights, and sweeping tailfins.

12
1968. By the late sixties, jet-inspired embellishments give way to a flowing aerodynamic shape with subtle sculptural details.

A GALLERY OF EUROPEAN AND AMERICAN CLASSIC CARS 1930-1946

During the period of the great classic automobiles, the design of cars achieved a remarkable harmony of line and refinement of detail. The automobile enjoyed a Golden Age. The belief that the car was the most desirable way to get around (at a time when the Sunday drive was still fun) was reflected in elegant and energetic forms that beautifully expressed the automobile's function. (Photographs by Alexandre Georges.)

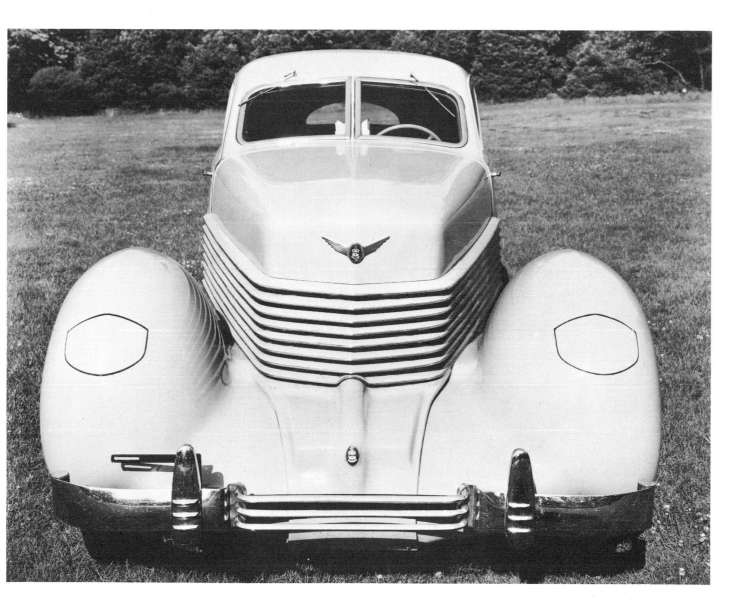

1
Talbot. 1939. (Model first produced in 1937.) France.

2
Bentley. 1939. Britain.

3
Cadillac 60 Special. 1939.

4
Lincoln Continental. 1941. (Model first produced in 1940.)

5
Jeep. 1951. (Model first produced in 1941.)

6
Cisitalia. 1949. (Model first produced in 1946.) Italy.

7
Cord. 1937.

Two classic grilles: the Mercedes-Benz (1930) and the Rolls-Royce. A car's grille is its most distinctive, easy-to-idenitfy feature. Over the years, the grille has come to play an almost purely decorative function as the true pop sculpture of our time. The two grilles pictured here show the elegance that can be achieved on the assembly line. The same basic designs — somewhat modified along aerodynamic lines — still grace the Mercedes and the Rolls (Photograph of the Mercedes-Benz by Alexandre Georges.)

Mercedes-Benz. 1930. Germany. (Photograph by Alexandre Georges.

Classic Rolls-Royce grille.

The Thunderbird (1955) and the MG, Mustang, and Jaguar (1960s) are four of the most popular sport cars designed in recent years. The "Bird" of the 1950s and the later "Horse" are the most successful and widely copied mass-produced sports cars in America.

Since the middle 1950s, the annual restyling of automobiles, as we have noted, has been strongly influenced by the soaring design of jet aircraft. As the illustrations here show, the effect of jet design on cars has produced some bizarre forms. In their imitation of aircraft, cars have sprouted chrome-embellished wings, tails, and jet engines. In a few instances whole planes have been reproduced on a miniature scale as fender and hood ornaments. (Photographs by Fortune Monte.)

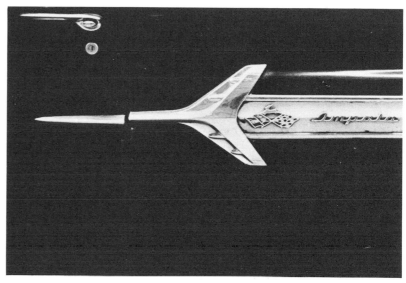

Each day every human being old enough to read and get about in the world is bombarded with thousands of graphic images in the form of magazine covers, illustrations, and advertisements, book jackets, billboards, packaging, posters, record-album covers, painted and electrified signs, TV graphics, and dozens of other word and picture messages. Unlike its cousins in the fine arts, painting and sculpture, which can be enjoyed from a relaxed, seated position, most graphic art is designed to catch the viewer on the run and make him do something: read a book, fly to Mexico, see a movie, buy a car. In recent years graphic design has come to play another important role: that of creating an imposing and respectable image for large corporations. Many major American companies have hired design specialists to update everything from their business cards and stationery to their corporate symbols. Two noteworthy examples of the latter are RCA and MGM, whose famous trademark monograms now reflect bold, identifiable-at-a-glance contemporary styling.

More than any other art medium, graphic design is the true expression of our age of exploding information and instant communication. Characteristic of our use-it-once-throw-it-away culture, most graphic design, while it may be reproduced in vast quantities, is remarkably short lived. After only a few seconds or, at most, a month of exposure, the television title and magazine illustration pass into oblivion. In spite of this impermanence, however, the fast-growing field of graphic design commands many of the brightest and most inventive talents in art.

Posters

Nowhere is the new wave of graphic design more strik-ing than in the burgeoning world of posters. Not since the great poster artists of the late nineteenth and early twentieth centuries, innovators such as Toulouse-Lautrec, the Czech Alphonse Mucha, and America's Edward Penfield, has this ancient medium of communication seen such a flowering. In addition to their traditional function of announcing events such as movies, plays, and concerts, selling consumer products, and promoting travel, posters are fast becoming an independent medium of graphic art in their own right. From coast to coast, and seemingly overnight, dozens of small stores which sell nothing but posters have sprung up. Many of the designs, like the kaleidoscopic, eye-popping psychedelic posters, are conceived as mass-produced works of art, containing no message apart from their own colorful images.

Chief among the designers who have revolutionized the once dying poster field are Milton Glaser, Peter Max, and the young Japanese artist, Yokoo. All of them have exhibited in poster shows at New York's Museum of Modern Art; some of their designs, like Glaser's famous poster for Simon and Garfunkel, have become collector's items. Many contemporary fine artists known chiefly for their work in other media, such as pop painter Roy Lichtenstein and sculptor Ernest Trova, have tried their hands successfully at poster design.

Illustration

For decades, magazine illustration has been one of the most popular and exacting areas of graphic design. Like designs for book jackets and record-album covers, magazine illustrations have the special obligation of complementing the material — story or article — they accompany. Early in the twentieth century, and well into the thirties, illustrators for magazines included many illustrious names whose styles were instantly identifiable: Howard Pyle, James Montgomery Flag, Maxfield Parrish, N. C. Wyeth, John Held, Jr., Harold Von Schmidt, and Norman Rockwell, to name just a few. From the late thirties until the middle of the 1950s — with a few notable exceptions — magazine illustration suffered the decline general to most fields of graphic art. Designs became pallid and fussily realistic, or so sentimental and idealized that the heroes and heroines of popular fiction looked like empty-headed members of the same cheerful, square-jawed family. The art of the magazine illustrator had become a minor adjunct to the writer's story rather than serious and compelling work with its own merit.

By the middle fifties, however, a few far-sighted magazine editors came to realize the increasing need for good graphic design and illustration. Art directors were given greater control over the appearance and editorial content of magazines, from logo and cover design to type and page layout, as well as greater autonomy in the choice of outstanding — and often very young — photographers and illustrators. The result was a renaissance in magazine design and, particularly, illustration. Among the artists — many of them trained in the fine arts — who helped to raise magazine illustration to a high level during this period are Robert Weaver, Tomi Ungerer, Harvey Schmidt, Bernard Fuchs, Milton Glaser, Tom Allen, Phil Hays, and Paul Davis. Although their styles are quite varied — ranging from complex, semi-abstract design to vigorous realism — they have in common great technical authority and an inventive and serious spirit usually associated only with the fine arts. As varied as the styles of these illustrators are the art di-

rectors and magazines who early encouraged their new and dynamic work. Among them are Bernard Quint (*Life*), Henry Wolfe and Robert Benton (*Esquire*), Otto Storch (*McCalls*), Richard Gangel (*Sports Illustrated*), and Leo Lionni (*Fortune*), as well as the editors of such less well-known but graphically daring publications as *The Lamp* (which is the company magazine of Standard Oil of New Jersey), the illustrated Annual Report of The Ansul Company of Wisconsin, and the CBS *Diary*.

The art directors named above, and a few others, realized that while the work of the illustrator and the writer must be mutually supporting, a good illustration, whatever its style, must have a significant life of its own and not act merely as a facile reflection of a story. While illustration continues on the high level established during the past decade or so, it must be added that magazines are turning more and more to photography and designs emphasizing lettering and eye-catching type faces. A parallel development is at work in the fine arts. Painters are abandoning the traditional techniques and media of the artist and, as in the case of pop art, turning to the tools and media of commercial reproduction, including, interestingly enough, photography, lettering, and type.

TV Graphics

The field of graphic art seen more often by more people than any other is design for television. The importance and impact of TV graphic art can be readily grasped when one realizes that (according to an article in the July 14, 1968, *New York Times Magazine*) the average child spends more time in front of the TV screen than with his teachers or parents, and that the average adult will pass from *ten to fifteen years* of his total life span watching television. Never has the designer been offered so vast an audience. At the same time, no other medium imposes such strict technical limitations on the designer. Even with the optimum reception of a studio monitor, the TV image lacks the clarity and sharpness of detail possible with a poster or magazine reproduction. In addition, as most veteran viewers know, the image on the average home set is even further reduced in sharpness much of the time because of poor reception and a host of other malfunctions and tuning problems.

Bearing these problems in mind — as well as the already-noted fact that his work, whether titles, credits, or graphic images, while seen by tens of millions, may be visible for just seconds — the designer of television graphics must produce work that is bold and free of details and nuances of tone. As the examples in this chapter indicate, the results can be both easy to grasp and beautiful. Like its close relative, graphic design for movies, design for television is an art that exists in a time sequence. Individual images reproduced as stills can only approximate the original effect achieved with dissolves, cuts, pans, and movement toward and away from the spectator. Using lettering, type, photography, animation, live action, painting, collage, and sometimes even three-dimensional constructions, the TV graphic designer has evolved a spare, imaginative style that has tremendously affected our ability to read and understand at a glance visual images and information in virtually every other area of art and communication.

Designs for posters, magazines, and television illustrate in their most characteristic forms — bold word-and-image message, painterly approach, and second-by-second changes of light pattern — the aesthetic range and technical variety found in today's graphic art. All other areas of graphic design, including advertising in its myriad forms (the design of shopping bags, menus, matchbook covers, and so on) use these techniques singly or in some combination. Even the examples of "folk" or "naive" graphic design reproduced on the following pages and created by unsophisticated and anonymous artists reveal the vigor and feeling for form and pattern that delight us in the work of today's professional designer.

1
Storyboard created by composer Harvey Schmidt for a musical play. The drawings, which depict a journey from the country into the city on New Year's Eve, are designed to be projected onto a cyclorama.

2
Nihon Electric Company advertising tower, Tokyo, Japan. The constantly changing electric patterns, designed by Kenji Ito, are shown here in nine of their stages. (Photographs by S. Kawai, Bijutsu Shuppan-sha.)

3
Animated figures designed in a loose, expressionistic style by Stanley Van Der Beek for the television camera.

4
Animated title sequence for television designed by Jerome Gask for ABC, Great Britain. (From *TV Graphics* by Roy Laughton. Published by Van Nostrand Reinhold Company, New York.)

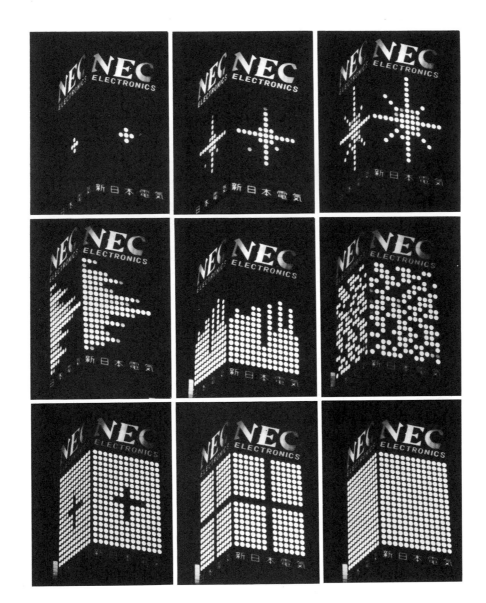

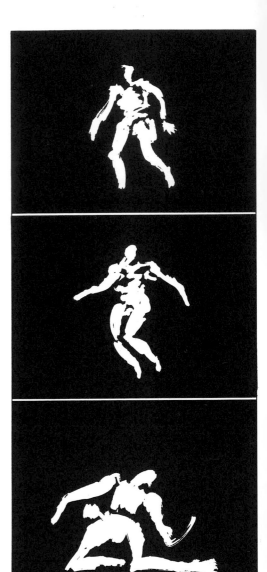

161

162

163

165

166

167

169

170

171

The eight posters on pages 102 to 105 reflect the variety of styles used by the contemporary designer to communicate in this traditional graphic medium.

5
Milton Glaser's striking poster announcing a Simon and Garfunkel concert combines an inventive three-dimensional alphabet with portraits of the artists designed in the same spirit.

6
Sculptor Ernest Trova gives his familiar helmeted, armless figure (see page 46) a graphic role: to repeat the square format of a poster announcing an exhibition of the artist's sculpture.

7
Pop artist Roy Lichtenstein combines his bold comic-strip style with "moderne" design and lettering elements recalling the twenties and thirties.

8 & 12
The Oriental Institute and "a" posters were designed for Chicago by Container Corporation of America as part of a program to call attention to the city's cultural and recreational facilities.

102

9
A limited edition, personal poster designed by Tadanori Yokoo and reproduced in silk screen. The rhythmic design combines autobiographical images with national symbols of Japan (including, in the upper left corner, the Tokaido Express).

10
Four-sheet poster designed by Milton Glaser to announce an Easter concert of gospel singer Mahalia Jackson. The four sheets combine to form a graphic bull's-eye.

11
Psychedelic poster by Peter Max using repeated and fragmented images like those produced by a kaleidoscope.

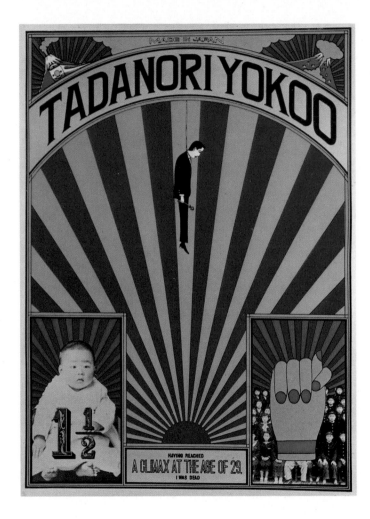

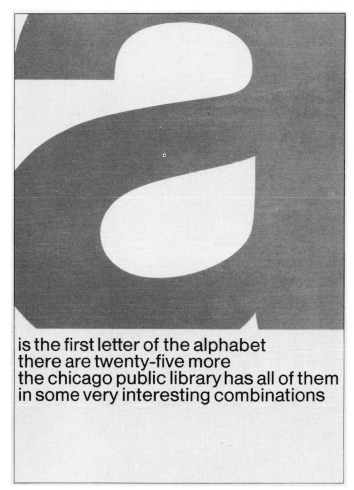

is the first letter of the alphabet
there are twenty-five more
the chicago public library has all of them
in some very interesting combinations

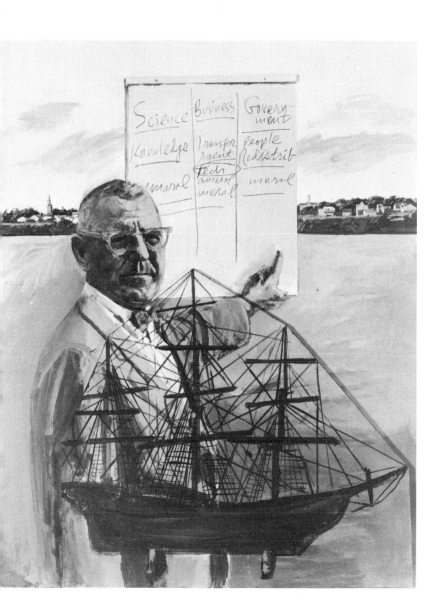

13, 14, 15
Three illustrations from the 1967 Annual Report of the Ansul Company by Robert Weaver.

One of the great illustrators of our time, Robert Weaver combines the painter's skill with the medium (in this instance acrylic paints) with the reporter's keen eye and ability to work accurately and quickly from life. Weaver describes his assignment briefly:

"I spent three or four days of undirected browsing, note taking, and sketching at Ansul's plant at Marinette, Wisconsin. Back in my studio in New York, I was faced with the problem of devising a workable and fresh approach (there is a different artist for each Annual Report) which would describe not only what goes on at the plant but something of the philosophy and thinking of its management. Both practical and abstract information had to be translated into visual language.

"All three pictures stay within the bounds of a single compositional arrangement, comparable to the stanza in poetry, while within each illustration there is the repetition of certain pictorial elements, like the use of rhyming. In the portrait of President Hood (right) the diagram he has just drawn echoes — in its pattern of vertical and horizontal lines — the rigging of the ship model, of which his office boasts a large collection. I have tried to show both captain of industry and idealistic teacher. The fire-protection instructor applying a torch to a demonstration wall (left) is linked visually by a planning sheet lettered in red to an employee applying a stencil to a freshly packed extinguisher. In the third illustration (center) I show by repeating as well as contrasting lines that there is a connection between green-house experiments with new herbicides and healthier crops."

16
Record jacket for a
Thelonius Monk album
designed for Columbia
Records by Paul Davis.

17
Four covers for *Graphis*,
the international maga-
zine for advertising and
graphic art. *Above left:*
Angel Grañena. *Above
right:* Tomi Ungerer. *Below left:* Etienne Delessert.
Below right: Flavio Con-
stantini. (The Graphis
Press.)

18
Illustration by
Bernard Fuchs for
Sports Illustrated.

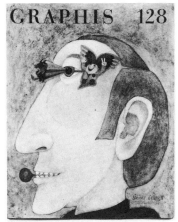

19
Album cover (and preliminary sketch) designed by Milton Glaser for Columbia Records.

20
Portrait of Mahalia Jackson designed by Tom Allen for Columbia Records.

21
Illustration by Philip Hays for *Esquire.*

111

22
Credits designed by Saul Bass for the movie *West Side Story*. This sequence recreates the film's New York slum environment by exploring brick walls, fences, doors, and signs, on which credits appear as scrawled and lettered graffiti.

23
Film credits designed by Stanley Van Der Beek from patterns made by a programmed computer.

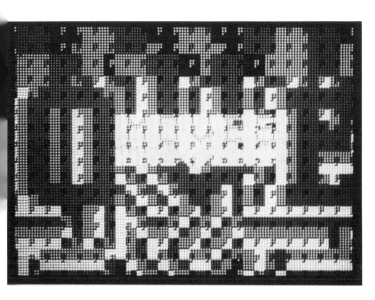 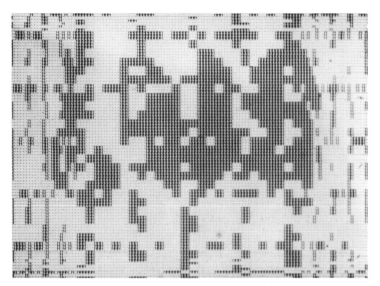

 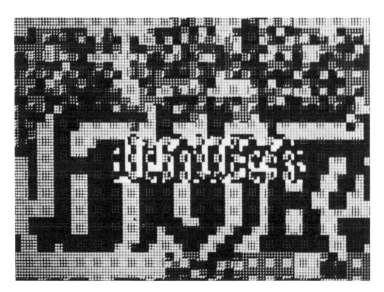

24
ABC television on-air logo.

25
One of the best-known symbols of our time, the CBS "eye." (Registered service mark of Columbia Broadcasting System, Inc.)

26
NBC television network on-air logo.

27
New trademark designed in 1967 for Radio Corporation of America.

28
Paper napkin, matchbook, and sugar-cube wrapper designed by Alexander Girard for L'Etoile restaurant, New York City. (de-Garmo McCaffery, Inc.)

29
Envelope for Push Pin Studios, Inc.

30
Title for the off-Broadway musical, *The Fantasticks*, designed by its composer, Harvey Schmidt.

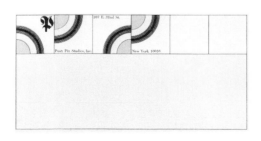

The Fantasticks

31
"Bill's Meat Market," window, a lively pop art assemblage of lettering, symbols, and images. (Photograph by Fortune Monte.)

32
Advertisement for Container Corporation of America. Albert Einstein's statement: "Perfection of means and confusion of goals seem — in my opinion — to characterize our age," has been interpreted by photographer-designer Art Kane as a sterile, alienated family of store dummies.

The energetic hard-sell world of Bill's Meat Market window, with its bold lettering, boxes with grinning faces, and jolly pig, is light years removed from the cool graphic elegance of Container Corporation's ad. Yet each projects an accurate and valid image of the company it advertises.

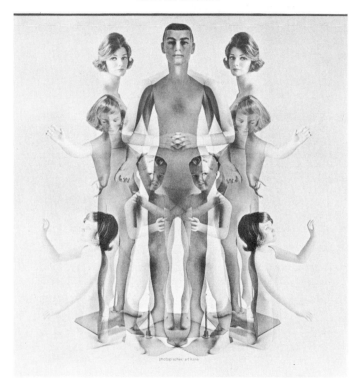

perfection of means and confusion of goals seem — in my opinion — to characterize our age

Breck Shampoo brings out the shine in your hair. Like brushing 100 strokes.

Of all the leading shampoos, only Breck does not have a synthetic detergent base.

Beautiful Hair
BRECK

YOUR HAIRDRESSER IS A PROFESSIONAL. ASK WHICH BRECK PREPARATIONS ARE BEST FOR YOUR HAIR.

33
Girl's face painted on the side of a bread delivery truck. (Photograph by Bill Berry.)

34
Advertisement for Breck shampoo. (John H. Breck Co., Division of American Cyanamid. Artist: Ralph William Williams.)

These images reflect two extremes in the use of art in modern advertising. The bright-eyed girl on the bread truck is drawn in the bold "shorthand" style of the comics. The huge, lash-fringed eyes, highlighted mouth, and mysteriously indicated nose project a mixed feeling, at once realistic and surrealistic. In vivid contrast to the pop art bread girl, Breck's smoothly modeled young lady painted in pastels represents a high degree of professional sophistication. Yet in its bland perfection it lacks altogether the graphic vigor of the crude image.

35
Paper bags designed by
Ivan Chermayeff for The
Museum of Modern Art.
(Black and white are
reversed here.)

8. Clothes: Contemporary Costume

Clothing today has become a means of vivid self-expression. An energetic underground movement in personal clothing is revolutionizing the world of dress — not just among the teen-agers who have created it, but in the aloof and conservative adult world of high fashion itself. A decade ago, a young couple strolling down the street with matching shoulder-length hairdos, World War I pilots' tunics, knee-high vinyl boots, and love beads would have been headed for a costume party. Today, in many cities, this couple could be reporting to a nine-to-five office job. Adults who are alarmed by the bizarre new styles in dress and adornment often end up wearing toned-down versions of them designed by the fashion industry for mass consumption.

The photographs in this chapter are a small survey of what is happening to clothing today. If one thing characterizes the fashion explosion of the past few years, it is the extraordinary diversity in personal dress one can see at a given moment on the street, in an office, or at a party. The wide-ranging variety of styles we find in the fine arts is reflected in clothing — with special emphasis on minimal designs, such as miniskirts, see-through clothing, and, again like painting and sculpture, a widespread use of the new materials of modern industry: plastics, paper, and even — in some far-out dresses — light-weight metals and glass and lights. Designers of clothes have borrowed, among other things, the dizzying patterns and strident colors of psychedelic art and the high-contrast colors and black-and-white patterns of op.

Most bizarre of all are the highly personalized clothes of the hippies. The "flower children" have introduced the revolutionary idea of borrowing from the past, not just the reinterpretation of historic styles one finds in high fashion but the use of old clothes themselves. While wearing secondhand dresses, jackets, vests, and coats may be bad news for the clothing industry, it has produced a flamboyant and eclectic style that combines elements from military uniforms, American Indian and cowboy outfits, and Italian and Oriental clothing with a flair for elegant shapes and profiles recalling the eighteenth century, Edwardian England, and the 1920s. As further embellishment, the hippies have revived the happy habit of bedecking themselves with flowers (sometimes plastic ones) and even feathers, as well as rings, beads, and medallions. The total effect, if it horrifies the more sedate members of the gray-flannel establishment, is bizarre and sometimes beautiful — a pop version of the individualistic young dandies of the Renaissance in Italy. With the hippy movement, fashion has gone full cycle to become contemporary costume. From their communities of self-imposed exile, notably Haight-Ashbury and East Village, the hippies have exercised a considerable influence on the clothing habits of much of the rest of the country. All large cities and most small ones boast "boutiques," which carry more sober versions of the designs created originally by the flower community.

Still photograph from Franco Zeffirelli's *Romeo and Juliet*, showing the full hair style and elegant attire of the fifteenth-century Italian male. (Copyright © 1968 by Paramount Pictures Corporation.)

Hippy clothes, with their variety of design and inventive details, are the costume symbols of our time among young people. (Designs by Dana; photographs by Fortune Monte.)

 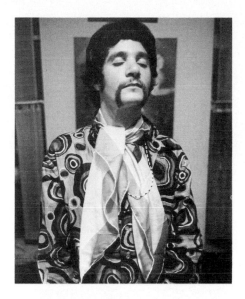 

3 & 4
Two versions of contemporary high fashion for men. The worried-looking mannequin from the window of Bonwit Teller sports an elegant model of the traditional business suit with added flair provided by a wide, figured tie and dark shirt. The dummy's heavily lined face helps the affluent shopper identify with the heavy burden that comes with money and success. The "Nehru" jacket on the living model, inspired by Oriental clothing, is replacing conventional lapels and tie among sophisticated dressers. The decorative pendant recalls the elegant jewelry worn by men in the Renaissance. (Bonwit Teller mannequin photograph by Fortune Monte; model photograph courtesy Alexander's Department Stores, New York.)

5
The businessman, front and rear. The standard dark suit, with its white shirt and narrow tie, is a modern office uniform designed for anonymity and tolerating few personal flights of fancy. (Photographs by Fortune Monte.)

6
Hair, always a major concern of fashion, has become in our time a symbol of social protest. The long and often dizzy-looking hair styles worn by hippies, rock groups, and many students may antagonize parents, teachers, and the barbers' union, but they have a long history in male fashion. (Photograph of Earth Opera courtesy Elektra Records.)

7
Store window dummy, a model of the modern young businessman. (Photograph by Fortune Monte.)

8 & 9
Contrasting clothes concepts of the modern man. At the left, the formal, conservative dark suit with a plain shirt and black tie, for office wear. On the right, vivid personal attire with printed fabric designs, flowers, and neckwear inspired by creative invention of hippies and flower children. (Photographs by Frederick W. Brink.)

10
This formal installation at The Metropolitan Museum of Art's exhibition, "The Art of Fashion," illustrates, on a small scale, the cool, detached world of contemporary high fashion for women, from beach wear and street dresses to elegant evening gowns. Even in the tradition-conscious world of high fashion there is remarkable diversity today in styles and materials; short skirts and pants in plain colors and rich patterns, solid and sheer stockings, shoes and boots, made from conventional fabrics and materials as well as the transparent and opaque plastics of modern industry. (The Metropolitan Museum of Art.)

11
From the ideal to the reality: fashion in the street. (Photograph by Fortune Monte.)

12
Cutouts by Alex Katz.
1966. Oil-painted alumi-
num and brass. (Fisch-
bach Gallery. Photograph
by Rudolph Burckhardt.)

13
Still photograph from
"2001: A Space Odyssey."

14
German tilting armor made by Anton Peffenhauser, Augsburg. 1580. (The Metropolitan Museum of Art, The Bashford Dean Memorial Collection, Gift of Helen Fahnstock Hubbard, 1929, in memory of her father, Harris C. Fahnstock.)

15
Apollo A6L pressure suit (front and back). (National Aeronautics and Space Administration.)

16
Heated diving suit. (Courtesy Marine Contracting International, Inc.)

17
Two-hundred-pound anti-bomb flak suit. (Courtesy GAF Corporation.)

18
Paper coverall. (Mr. Fashion Seal Uniforms, Huntington, N.Y. From "Made with Paper," Museum of Contemporary Crafts. Photograph by Ferdinand Boesch.)

Protective clothing reflects the needs peculiar to the period in history during which it is designed. The armored suit was developed during the Middle Ages as protection in battle against arrows and crude hand weapons. With

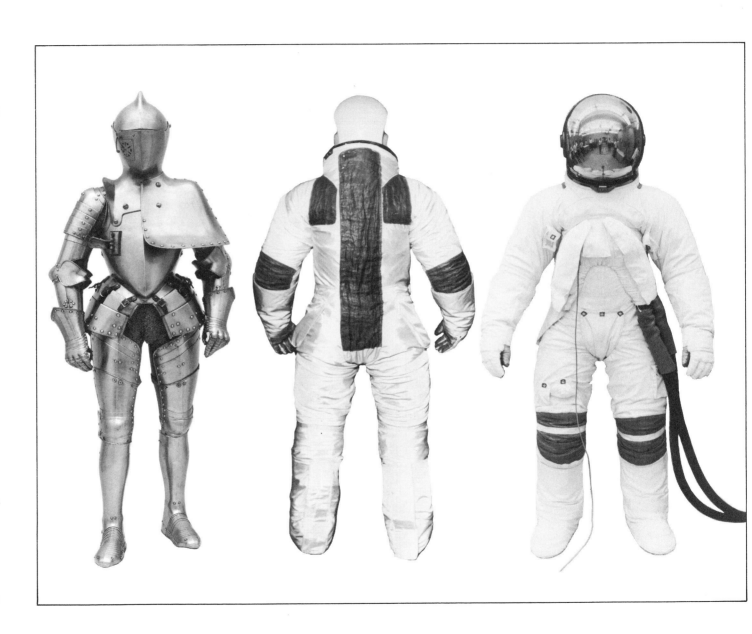

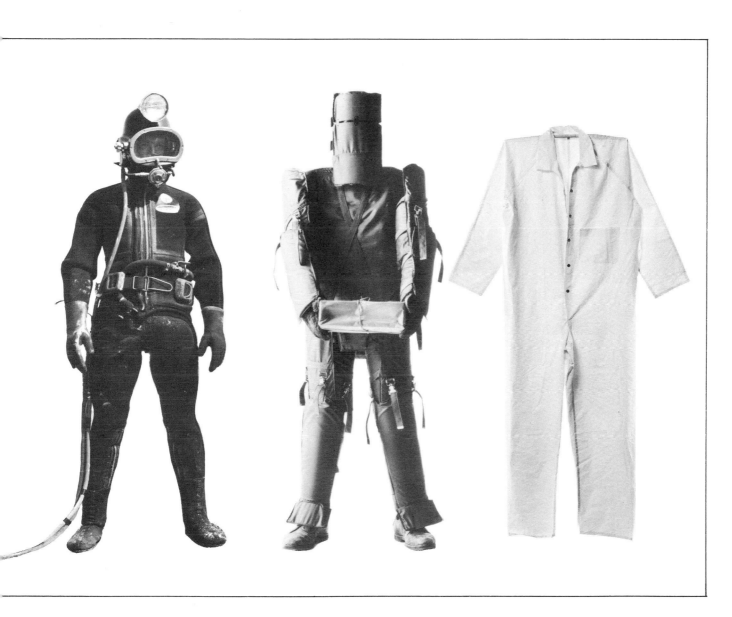

the invention of gunpowder, armor lost its protective function and became a form of ceremonial dress.

The Apollo pressure suit, while it lacks the dashing style of the armor, serves a far more sophisticated protective function: it is designed to be worn on space missions during prelaunch and launch phases and during re-entry.

The modern heated diving suit is designed to protect its wearer from cold and water pressure and, like the Apollo suit, to provide for normal breathing in an environment without oxygen.

The anti-bomb suit, with its protective shielding around torso and limbs and slit-eyed helmet, looks like a space-age version of Frankenstein's monster.

The paper coverall, a delicate and innocent form compared with the other protective garments, is just as symbolic of our time: it is designed to protect the wearer from everyday dirt, and it can be thrown away.

The design of uniforms is the most inflexible and traditional in clothing. It is also frequently the most beautiful. Some uniforms, like Michelangelo's designs for the Vatican's Swiss guards and the habits of many religious orders, have remained virtually unchanged for hundreds of years. Uniforms are designed to perform very special functions: chiefly, to standardize individual appearance and to project a formal, authoritative, and imposing image.

19
Mounted police, New York City.

20
Motorcycle police, New York City. (Photographs courtesy Bureau of Public Information. Police Department, New York City.)

21
Policemen, Rome, Italy. (Photograph by John Bennett Dobbins.)

22
U.S. Army enlisted uniform. (U.S. Army Photograph.

23
Camouflage uniform of Special Forces troops. (U.S. Army Photograph.)

The unofficial self-styled uniform is a special feature of clothing today. It is most often associated with motorcycle clubs and, in a more fanciful form, with rock and folk music groups. The world of speed and leather of the "bike" riders is closely identified with recklessness and crude masculinity.

24
Denim, vinyl, and leather are the tough materials of the motorcycle rider. The lettered jacket with its lively, wicked image and the crash helmets call to mind the headgear and symbolic colors of medieval warriors. (Photograph by Jay F. Good.)

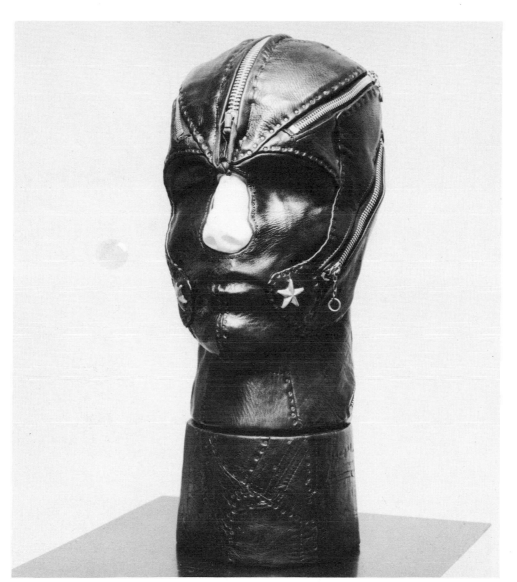

25 & 26
Leather masked heads by Nancy Grossman. The eyes and mouths of these frightening heads are sealed behind leather. Metal rings, studs, stars, and zippers produce a feeling of restraint and torture. The cult of un-emotional detachment is carried to an extreme in these multi-media sculptures. (Cordier & Ekstrom, Inc., New York. Photographs by Geoffrey Clements.)

27
Wig in a store window. (Photograph by Fortune Monte.)

28
No by Richard Lindner.
1966. Oil on canvas.

29
Rock-Rock by Richard
Lindner. 1966. Oil on canvas. Contemporary cloth-
ing as the theme of pop
art. Lindner's flashy paintings catch the dynamic
and exaggerated spirit of
today's clothing in a
leggy, aggressive female
swinger and a wiggy-
looking rock idol with an
electric-guitar torso.
(Cordier & Ekstrom, Inc.,
New York. Photographs by
Geoffrey Clements.)

During every period in the long history of man, the complex structures designed by architects have been vivid symbols of the spirit and life of the times.

Modern buildings, whether they appear in Los Angeles, Milan, Tokyo, or Caracas, loom in similar forms, reflecting both the genius of twentieth-century technology and our frequent lack of creative individualism. Contemporary architecture is a fascinating combination of advanced technology and a strong symbol of the functions and desires of people today. Concrete, steel, and glass are among the chief materials of the modern builder. One result is soaring structures impossible at other periods. The simplest structures and the most complex, from the drive-in hot-dog stand to the skyscraper, require the knowledge and skills of practiced engineers if they are to fulfill their functions successfully. Like design in general today, in painting, clothing design, and graphic art, there is a frequent reliance on severity and repetition in architecture. As the average city dweller may realize every day, office buildings, apartment houses, factories, and even schools, while quite different in function, are often related in design by massive, bold outline and repetitious, plain surface. At their best, as some of the examples reproduced in this chapter indicate, contemporary buildings can be refined and elegant, with subtle and visually compelling materials and design. At its worst, modern architecture can be boring.

The buildings, structures, and details on the following pages are examples of architectural forms, several designed by leading architects of this century, daily confronted by millions of people. Two are perfect symbols of our time: the towering commercial office building and the airport terminal. Each reflects clearly our deep concern with the life of business, from insuranc to television, and our reliance on jet transportatior Many of the most highly regarded and inventive moc ern architects have been called upon to design th office buildings and airport terminal shown here. Mos of the other examples, such as the museum, universit library, school, and factories, illustrate the remarkabl similarity in widely diverse functions dictated by moc ern technology and taste. The structures reproducec here are mainly of the past ten years. Details of interi ors have been included to show the occasional coop eration of architects with sculptors and painters.

1-5
The bold, often severe, form of modern architecture is most clearly revealed in soaring commercial skyscrapers and sprawling apartment houses. The examples on pages 143-144 show two American skyscrapers and the apartment structure at Montreal's Expo 67. They also include other varied but highly expressive modern symbols, a school and a museum. In spite of their widely varied functions, the skyscrapers, apartment house, museum, and school have much in common and reflect clearly the age they represent. They are severe and impersonal, technically powerful but occasionally monotonous.

1
Seagram Building, New York City, 1958, by Ludwig Mies van der Rohe. (Photograph by Jane Dogett and Malcolm Smith.)

2
Chicago Civic Center by Skidmore, Owings & Merrill. (Photograph courtesy of Bill Engdahl, Hedrich Blessing.)

3
The Whitney Museum.
New York City, 1966, by
Marcel Breuer.

4
Woodrow Wilson High
School, Los Angeles, by
Paul R. Williams and
Associates. (Photograph
courtesy Los Angeles
Board of Education.)

5
"Habitat" at Expo 67,
Montreal.

CBS 52

6-16
One of the most solid
and impressive recent
skyscrapers in New York
City is the CBS Building,
designed by Eero Saarinen
and built in 1964. The
towering exterior is a
visually compelling con-
trast of soaring piers of
dark gray granite and
transparent glass win-
dows. The details of the
interior reproduced here
illustrate the familiar
forms encountered and
used daily by thousands
of employees in modern
commercial buildings in
countless cities. In the
CBS Building, in addition
to elevators, control panels, and mail boxes, is a
large number of designs
such as decorative wall
panels using raised lettering and metal plates,
which symbolize the func-
tions of the building and
its offices and extend to
employees and visitors
personal and absorbing
visual design concepts.

6
The CBS building.

7, 8, 9
Details of the exterior.

10
Ground floor elevators.

11
Elevator panel.

12
Office directory.

13
Viewing room wall detail.

14
Relief sculpture and
graphic art on lunch room
wall.

15
Mail chute.

16
Lunch room.

Factories, and related
structures, are among the
most symbolic buildings
of the modern age. One
of the chief concerns of
our time and a great
source of money and
power is mass-manufac-
turing. The illustrations
on pages 149-150 show
buildings designed for
IBM, producer of a wide
and widely used range of
information handling de-
vices. In addition to plants,
there are research cen-
ters and laboratories, in
Europe and America. Be-
sides the usual severity
and design repetition of
contemporary commercial
buildings (as well as contemporary schools), these
examples show instances
of design imagination
which call to mind the
manipulation of form and
space by the sculptor —
notably the pier supports
of the laboratory at La-
Gaude, France, the work
of Marcel Breuer and
Associates.

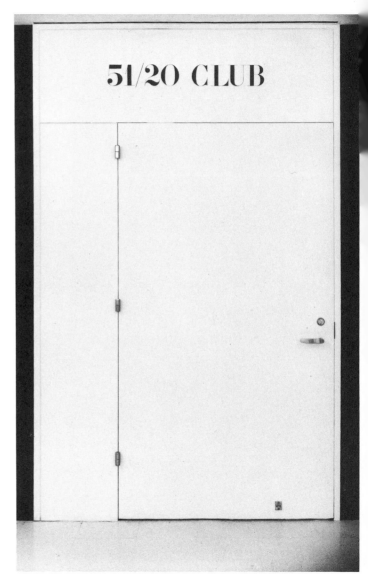

18
IBM laboratory, East Fish-kill, New York. Architect: Paul Rudolph and Associates. (Photograph courtesy Scott d'Arazien, Inc.)

17
IBM plant, Rochester, Minnesota, Architect: Eero Saarinen & Associates. (Photograph by Ezra Stoller Associates.)

19
IBM Research center, Yorktown, New York. Architect: Eero Saarinen & Associates. (Photograph courtesy Ezra Stoller.)

20
IBM laboratory, Boeblingen, Germany. Architect: K. A. Oppenhofer. (IBM Pressfoto.)

21
Detail of IBM laboratory
at LaGaude, France.

22
IBM laboratory, LaGaude,
France. Architect: Marcel
Breuer & Associates.

23-28
The commercial jet airplane (discussed in Chapter 1) is the most widely experienced and vivid example of the advanced technology of modern transportation. Airport architecture is frequently among the most inventive and visually fascinating of modern design. The reproductions on pages 151-152 show exterior and interior views of the TWA Building at Kennedy Airport, New York City, designed by Eero Saarinen and Associates and built in 1962. Unlike the massive, rectangular slabs of most of today's office buildings and apartment houses, Saarinen's glass and concrete structure has a curvilinear, organic form. It expresses the technological range of modern architecture as well as a regard for visual variety. Both the exterior form of the building and details of the interior express an almost sculptural awareness of form and shape. (Photographs courtesy Ezra Stoller Associates.)

The interiors of a few modern buildings are greatly enhanced by the inclusion of sculpture, painting, and inlaid wall designs by leading contemporary artists. In this way the technical and aesthetic skills of architects and artists can be combined to produce deeply satisfying visual results. The examples reproduced here are from two landmark skyscrapers in New York City, the Pan American Building, designed by Emery Roth and Sons, and opened in 1963, and the Time & Life Building, designed by Harrison, Abramovitz, and Harris, and finished in 1959. One other example is from the Manufacturers Hanover Trust Company Building on Fifth Avenue. These are outstanding works of art, which offer a varied contrast to most severe and plain office building interiors.

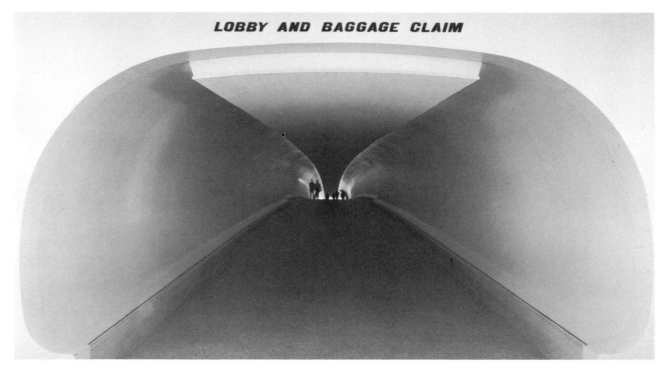

LOBBY AND BAGGAGE CLAIM

29
Aluminum and steel wall
sculpture by Gyorgy Kepes
in the Pan American
Building. (Photograph
courtesy J. Alex Langley.)

30
Portals, glass and metal
mural by Josef Albers in
the lobby of the Time &
Life Building. (Photograph
courtesy Impact Photos
Inc.)

31
Relational Painting #88,
oil on canvas mural by
Fritz Glarner in the lobby
of the Time & Life Build-
ing.

32
Detail of a sculptured
bronze screen by Harry
Bertoia from Manufac-
turers Hanover Trust
Company. (Photograph
courtesy Ezra Stoller.)

33-36
The structures on this and the following page represent four important aspects of contemporary American architecture. They are a detail of a commercial office building, a university library, a monument and stadium, and the stage of a famous theater. The contrast of business, education, history, and entertainment is symbolic of life today. Each function is a challenge to the technical and design creativity of the modern architect.

Detail of the facade supports of the American Republic Insurance Company in Des Moines, Iowa, by Skidmore, Owings & Merrill and completed in 1965. (Photograph courtesy Ezra Stoller.)

Beinecke Rare Book and Manuscript Library, Yale University, by Skidmore, Owings & Merrill and completed in 1963. (Photograph courtesy Ezra Stoller.)

Gateway Arch and Busch Memorial Stadium in St. Louis. The 630-foot arch, the nation's tallest monument, was designed by Eero Saarinen and erected in 1966. The stadium is by Edward D. Stone and was built in 1967. (Photograph courtesy The Chamber of Commerce of Metropolitan St. Louis.)

The stage of New York's Radio City Music Hall, designed by Rockefeller Center, Inc. Architects, and completed in 1932. (Photograph courtesy Radio City Music Hall.)

DATE DUE